An Interdisciplinary Bibliography

on Nationalism,

1935-1953

Karl W. Deutsch

Professor of History and Political Science

Massachusetts Institute of Technology

The Technology Press of M.I.T.

Cambridge

1956

CONTENTS

INTRODUCTION

The bibliography that follows has been organized from the point of view of the unity of science. This viewpoint was not brought to it as a preconceived notion. Rather, it grew from the experience of conducting research involving problems of nationalism and nationality.

In this research it became very soon apparent that no single scientific discipline nor any single branch of humanistic scholarship was sufficient to deal with the problem. The analytical social sciences seemed shallow without the large processes and long series of data that are recorded by history. Yet history seemed vague or chaotic without the help of the more analytic disciplines. All of the social sciences, on occasion, required specific data, or even general answers, from various natural sciences, ranging from geography and biology to the more recent studies of communication and control.

Other investigators may feel that either more or fewer disciplines should have been included; that more weight should have been given to substantive data, or conversely, to mathematics and methodology; and they may feel that communication theory has either more, or less, of a contribution to offer for problems of nationalism and international relations than it has seemed to me.

Such objections are difficult to answer. The present bibliography originally grew out of the writing of a book, Nationalism and Social Communication, which was published in 1953 by the Technology Press of the Massachusetts Institute of Technology and John Wiley and Sons, Inc. One way of judging the viewpoint of this bibliography would be to examine the theories in the book that have been produced with its aid. But perhaps a better way of judging this viewpoint - and perhaps more broadly the viewpoint of the unity of science, as applied to the social sciences, - might simply be to look at the possible usefulness of this bibliography for other workers in the field.

Dr. Koppel Pinson's excellent "A Bibliographical Introduction to Nationalism" was published in 1935. Since that time there has been no comparable major attempt to survey the literature of the subject; the important surveys by Dr. Boyd Shafer and by Professor Louis Snyder deal with more limited topics. At the same time, the years from 1935 to 1953 have been unusually rich in significant publications in this field, and major advances have been made in the social sciences, both in the methods and findings within each special discipline, as well as in the extent and level of inter-disciplinary cooperation.

The present bibliography is divided into fourteen sections. Of these, the first lists a few major surveys and special bibliographies. The second section lists special works on nationalism. The eleven following sections list relevant books and articles by special fields. The last section - the fourteenth - is the longest. It lists books and

articles on nationalism by geographic area, subdivided for each area
by topics or fields of study in the same sequence as the listing of fields
in the preceding eleven sections.

Even as regards its central topic of nationalism this bibliography is selective, not complete. It is even more selective - and far
more incomplete - in its listings of materials from other sciences.
The test for inclusion or exclusion of each item has been usefulness.
Did it contain factual data, or did it contain some suggestions or ideas,
which seemed important enough to deserve consideration in the search
of a clearer understanding of nationalism or nationality? Occasionally,
I have included references to work still in progress, when it seemed
likely to continue some important investigation, or the train of thought
of a significant writer.

As new books and articles appeared during the compilation of
this bibliography from 1951 to 1955, I have tried to include those that
came to my attention and seemed particularly relevant to the purpose
of the work at hand. The bibliography should cover, therefore, a fair
part of the more important publications on nationalism through 1953,
with inclusions tapering off during the latter year to a few sporadic
items listed thereafter. A more thorough bibliography of works on
nationalism from 1952 onward will have to be undertaken several years
from now, when the harvest of more recent publications will have been
stored and indexed properly in libraries and catalogs, and when there
will have been more time for its evaluation. At present, relative com-
pleteness on the scale of the earlier years, or even a representative
balance of selections, seemed unattainable, but I tried to include some
of the livelier items of recent research in the hope of making the whole
bibliography more useful and more relevant to current research interests.

There are doubtlessly many items which should have been
included and are not. No omission of a book or article should be con-
sidered, therefore, as evidence of any adverse value judgement of its
contents; rather, it is evidence of the limitations of the compiler.

It should not be necessary to point out that listing a book or
article in this bibliography does not necessarily mean any endorsement
of the philosophical or political views of its author.

As mentioned above, the last section, number fourteen, is further subdivided by geographic areas. In the choice of these areas I have
followed, with some modifications, the subdivisions in Mr. Pinson's
earlier bibliography. None of these area listings can pretend in any
manner to represent bibliographies for area studies. The only purpose
of listing them has been to indicate books or articles that illustrate
problems of nationalism in general, even though their subject matter
happens to be drawn from some particular region. Taken all together,
they may illustrate the author's view that material for the study of
nationalism should be drawn from the West as well as from the East,

and from the old world as well as from the new. For any reasonably balanced or representative bibliography on area problems as such, however, readers will have to turn elsewhere.

When all is said and done, a bibliography is not a bible. It pretends to no authority either explicit or implied. The comments I have added to a number of items in the first three sections are notes from a workshop, not pronouncements ex cathedra. At best, a bibliography may serve men as a storehouse and a chest of tools from which each must select for himself those items best suited to his work. If some items in this collection should stimulate other investigators to fruitful disagreement, or if this list should help them to take into account some relevant facts, questions, or methods which otherwise might not have come so soon to their attention, it will have fulfilled its primary purpose. If it does fulfill that purpose, it may at the same time have demonstrated something of the usefulness of the viewpoint of the unity of science, and of the work of the Institute for the Unity of Science under whose sponsorship it was compiled.

In addition to the Institute, I am indebted for encouragement and advice to more individuals than I can list. Among the most helpful of all have been Frederick Bodmer, Rupert Emerson, Phillip Frank, Roman Jakobson, Hans Kohn, Margaret Mead, and Norbert Wiener. Without the help of my research assistant, Mrs. Hannelore Vanderschmidt, and without the patience and cooperation of the library staffs at the Massachusetts Institute of Technology, Harvard University, and the Babson Institute of Business Administration this bibliography could not have been completed.

Karl W. Deutsch

Massachusetts Institute of Technology
April 2, 1956

Note: A few items have been repeated from Dr. K.S. Pinson's Bibliographical Introduction to Nationalism. These are marked with the letter P.

BIBLIOGRAPHY ON NATIONALISM

1. ## SOME GENERAL BIBLIOGRAPHIES AND SURVEYS

1.1 Pinson, Koppel S., A Bibliographical Introduction to National-ism. New York, Columbia University Press, 1935. A selected and critically annotated bibliography.

1.2 Lasswell, Harold D., Ralph D. Casey and Bruce Lannes Smith, Propaganda, Communication and Public Opinion: A Compre-hensive Reference Guide. Princeton, Princeton University Press, 1946.

1.3 - - - Propaganda, and Promotional Activites: An Annotated Bibliography. Minneapolis, University of Minnesota Press, 1935.

1.4 Jahoda, Marie, Morton Deutsch and Stuart W. Cook, Research Methods in Social Relations with Especial Reference to Preju-dice. New York, Dryden Press, 1951, 2 vols. A valuable survey of research methods with many examples from the area of group tensions. Extensive bibliography.

1.5 Klineberg, Otto, Tensions Affecting International Understanding: A Survey of Research. New York, Social Science Research Council, 1950. A critical survey of research in anthropology and social psychology, mostly from 1920 to 1949, made in con-nection with the UNESCO project on International Tensions. Summarizing and evaluating well above 200 original research contributions, it represents "an imaginative and technically skillful ordering and application of scattered and fragmentary products of research on human behavior . . . . It does not pro-fess definitiveness for existing research techniques, yet it establishes their utility . . . Dr. Klineberg has given form and direction to a previously unstructured area of social knowledge" (Donald Young).

1.6 Kohn Hans, The Idea of Nationalism: A Study in Its Origins and Background. New York, Macmillan, 1944. The best his-torical survey stressing the history of nationalistic ideas.

1.7 Mead, Margaret, "National Character," in A. L. Kroeber Ed., Anthropology Today: An Encyclopedic Inventory, Chicago, University of Chicago Press, 1953, pp. 642-667.

1.8 - - - "The Study of National Character," in D. Lerner and H. D. Lasswell Eds., The Policy Sciences, Recent Developments in Scope and Method, Stanford University, Stanford University Press, 1951, pp. 70-86. A survey of recent anthropological research applied to nations.

1.9 Royal Institute of International Affairs, Nationalism (Chairman: E. H. Carr). London, Oxford University Press, 1939. A report by a study group of members of the Institute, and the best short qualitative survey of nationalism.

1.10 Shafer, Boyd C., Nationalism: Myth and Reality. New York, Harcourt, Brace and Co., 1955. " . . . an inquiry based on 20 years of reading and reflection into the meaning of nationalism," offering an excellent survey of recent historical research.

1.11 Snyder, Louis L., The Meaning of Nationalism. New Bruns- wick, Rutgers University Press, 1954. A very helpful survey of recent approaches to nationalism, surveying the contributions of the different disciplines of history and social science.

1.12 United Nations Commission on Human Rights, Definition and Classification of Minorities (Memorandum Submitted by the Secretary-General). (Lake Success, N. Y., 1950; U.N. Publi- cations, Sales No.: 1950. XIV. 3.) "Selected Bibliography," pp. 26-51.

1.13 United Nations Commission on Human Rights, The Main Types and Causes of Discrimination (Memorandum Submitted by the Secretary-General). (Lake Success, N. Y., 1949; U.N. Publi- cations, Sales No.: 1949. XIV. 3.) "Selected Bibliography on Discrimination and Related Subjects," pp. 58-88. Very help- ful for definitions and terminology. The term "minority" in- cludes "instances in which the numerical majority of the population, whether homogeneous or composed of differentiated groups, is in the position of a minority, the State being dom- inated by a numerically smaller group which imposes its own language, culture, etc."

1.14 Van Wagenen, Richard W., Research in the International Organi- zation Field, Some Notes on a Possible Focus. Publication No. 1 of the Center for Research on World Political Institutions, Princeton University, Princeton, New Jersey, 1952.

1.15 Wheare, K. C., Federal Government, 3rd Ed. New York, Oxford University Press, 1953. A comparative survey of the workings of federal government in several countries, the general conditions necessary for its success, and the prospects for its future development.

1.16 Williams, Robin, Jr., The Reduction of Intergroup Tensions: A Survey of Research on Problems of Ethnic, Racial and Religious Group Relations. New York, Social Science Research Council, 1947, Bulletin 57. "A report prepared for the Social Science Research Council . . . committee on techniques for reducing group hostility, (examining) the more important techniques and procedures in use by representative action agencies which are seeking to reduce hostility and resolve conflict in inter- racial and intercultural group relations" in the United States.

1.17 Woytinsky, W. S. and E. S. Woytinsky, World Population and Production. New York, Twentieth Century Fund, 1954.

1.17a   Wright, Quincy, W. F. Cottrell, C. H. Boasson and Ingemund Gullvåg, Research for Peace. Published for the Institute for Social Research, Oslo, North-Holland Publishing Co., Amsterdam, 1954. Prize winning contributions to an international contest.

1.18   Wright, Quincy, A Study of War. Chicago, University of Chicago Press, 1942. 2 vols. This monumental work contains a very large amount of material based on a thorough survey of the literature of the different social sciences before 1940. Nationalism is treated in chapters 26-28, public opinion and war in chapter 30, and the measurement of international relations in chapter 35. There are many simple quantitative data on the number of wars, casualties, etc., and much excellent material in 40 appendices, especially on "the definition of certain sociological terms" (in appendix 35).

1.19   - - - "The World Community." Chicago, University of Chicago Press, 1943. A series of papers and discussions held at the Harris Institute at the University of Chicago in 1947 bringing together historians, economists, political scientists, sociologists and anthropologists. Contains an inconclusive but helpful discussion of terminology, and useful papers by Louis Wirth, Margaret Mead, Kenneth E. Boulding, Robert C. Angell, Harold D. Lasswell and Pitman B. Potter.

1.20   Znaniecki, Florian, Modern Nationalities: A Sociological Study. Urbana, Illinois, University of Illinois Press, 1952. A brief qualitative summary of traditional sociological findings.

2. GENERAL WORKS ON NATIONALISM

2.1   Akzin, B., M. Ancel, Mirkine-Guetzevitch and J. Ray, La nationalité dans la science sociale et le droit contemporain. Paris, 1933.

2.2   Arnold, G. L., "Nationalism," Twentieth Century, Vol. 145, May 1949, pp. 261-271

2.3   Barker, Sir Ernest, National Character and the Factors in Its Formation. London, Harper 1927. P.

2.4   Basadre, J., "Why Nationalism," Americas, Vol. 1, Sept. 1949, pp. 12-14.

2.5   Batten, Edward, Nationalism: Politics and Economics. London, P. S. King, 1929.

2.6   Bauer, Otto, Die Nationalitaetenfrage und die Sozialdemokratie, 2nd Ed. Vienna, Volksbuchhandlung, 1924. P. A well-known study by the leading theorist of the democratic socialists in Austria.

2.7   Bay, (Jens) Christian, Ingemund Gullvåg, Harold Ofstad and Herman Tonessen, Nationalism: A Study of Identifications with People and Power: I. Problems and Theoretical Framework. Oslo, Institute for Social Research, June 1950 (mimeographed). Contains a bibliography pp. 62-67 and a list of 63 hypotheses to be tested by future research.

2.8   Berdyaev, N., "Attitudes toward the Revolution; Evolution of Nationalism and of Internationalism," Commonweal, Vol. 42 Sept. 28, 1945, pp. 570-572.

2.9   Bielstein, H. H. "Neue Männer -- Neue Bewegungen," Westermanns Monatshefte, Vol. 163, pp. 437-439; Vol. 164, pp. 29-32, 154-156, Feb., April 1938. Short reports from Nazi point of view about the nationalist parties of Leon Degrelle, Belgium; Rolf Henne, Switzerland; Dr. Oliveira Salazar, Portugal; Adam Koc, Poland; and the Cuza-Goga party of Roumania.

2.10 Bloom, Solomon, F., The World of Nations: A Study of the National Implications in the Work of Karl Marx. New York, Columbia University Press, 1941. A rich source of citations illustrating Marx' broad theory of nations, as well as its changing applications to day to day affairs.

2.11 Braunthal, Julius, The Paradox of Nationalism. London, St. Botolph, 1946. A slender survey, containing many telling examples of the illogicality of nationalist sentiment and of its easy manipulation by special interests and governments.

2.12 Brogan, D. W., "Power of Nationalism," New Republic, Vol. 109 Dec. 27, 1943, pp. 916-918.

2.13   Butler, Sir Harold, "Nationalism and the Western Tradition," in The Western Tradition. London, Vox Mundi, 1949, pp. 73-77.

2.14   Carr, Edward H., Nationalism and After. New York, Macmillan, 1945. The first chapter offers in less than 40 pages the best summary presentation of the profound social, economic and psychological changes in nationalism during the last 400 years, culminating in the "socialized nation" of present day politics and warfare.

2.15   Clark, George Norman, Unifying the World. London, Swarthmore Press, 1920.

2.16   Cobban, Alfred, National Self-Determination. London, Oxford University Press, 1945. A plea for "cultural autonomy" as an alternative to political succession using some of the arguments of Friedrich Meinecke.

2.17   Delos, Joseph T., La Nation. Montreal, Editions de l' Arbre, 1944. The work of a leading Roman Catholic scholar.

2.18   Deutsch, Karl W., Nationalism and Social Communication. New York, John Wiley, and Cambridge, Massachusetts Institute of Technology Press, 1953.

2.19   - - - "The Growth of Nations: Some Recurrent Patterns of Political and Social Integration," World Politics, Vol. 5, No. 2, Jan. 1953, pp. 168-195.

2.20   - - - "Nationalistic Responses to Study Abroad," Report of the Conference on International Educational Exchanges and Annual Meeting, the National Association of Foreign Student Advisers, East Lansing, Michigan, April 1952, pp. 9-20.

2.21   Dillard, H. C., "Nationalism: Mid-century Puzzle," Virginia Quarterly Review, Vol. 28 No. 4, Oct. 1952, pp. 532-546.

2.22   Earle, Edward Mead, ed., Nationalism and Internationalism: Essays Inscribed to Carlton J. H. Hayes. New York, Columbia University Press, 1950. Note particularly the essays on national poets by Jacques Barzun, and on Scandinavian problems by John Wuorinen.

2.23   Ehrmann, H. W., "Pre-Nationalism," New Republic, Vol. 110, May 29, 1944, p. 741.

2.24   Finot, Jean, Les préjugés des races, 2nd Ed. Paris, Alcan, 1905.

2.25   Friedmann, W., "New Nationalism," Fortnightly, Vol. 163 (new series Vol. 157), Jan. 1945, pp. 27-34.

2.26   Hancock, William K., Politics in Pitcairn and Other Essays. London, Macmillan Co., 1947.

2.27   Hansen, H., "Idea and Origins of Nationalism," Survey Graphic, Vol. 33, May 1944, pp. 251-252.

2.28   Hayes, Carlton J. H., Essays on Nationalism. New York, Mac-
        millan, 1926. P.

2.29   - - - "Nationalism," International Conciliation, Vol. 369,
        April 1941, pp. 227-239.

2.30   Hertz, Friedrich O., Nationalgeist und Politik. Zürich, Europa
        Verlag, 1937.

2.31   - - - Nationality in History and Politics: A Study of the Psy-
        chology and Sociology of National Sentiment and Character.
        London, K. Paul, Trench, Trubner, 1944. A storehouse of
        material and a shrewd survey of theories of nationality.

2.32   - - - "War and National Character," Contemporary Review,
        Vol. 171, May 1947, pp. 274-281.

2.33   Hrdlicka, A., "Nationalism," American Mercury, Vol. 121,
        March 1936, p. 11.

2.34   Hula, E., "National Self-Determination Reconsidered," Social
        Research, Vol. 10, 1943, pp. 1-21.

2.35   Inge, W. R., "Nationalism and National Character," Quarterly
        Review, Vol. 277, July 1941, pp. 125-143.

2.36   Janowsky, Oscar I., Nationalities and National Minorities with
        Special Reference to East-Central Europe. New York, Mac-
        millan, 1945.   Foreword by James T. Shotwell.   An impor-
        tant comparative survey of historical and political conditions,
        including Switzerland, Austria, South Africa and the Soviet
        Union, rich in data and reference to specialized works. "Selected
        bibliography," pp. 196-207.

2.37   Kautsky, Karl, "Nationalitaet und Internationalitaet," Ergän-
        zungshefte zur neuen Zeit, No. 1, 1907-1908 (Jan. 18, 1908),
        Stuttgart, P. Singer, 1908. A prominent socialist critic of
        Otto Bauer, favoring national assimilation rather than cultural
        autonomy.

2.38   Keller, Hans, K.E.L., Der Kampf um die Völkerordnung. For-
        schungs und Werbebericht der Akademie für die Rechte der
        Volker und der Internationalen Arbeitsgeneinschaft der Nation-
        alisten. Berlin, F. Vahlen, 1939. A product of the Nazi campaign
        for winning the sympathy of disgruntled nationalistic groups in
        Europe.

2.39   - - - Das rechtliche Weltbild. Berlin, Batschari, 1935.

2.40   King, James C., Some Elements of National Solidarity. Chicago,
        University of Chicago Press, 1935. An elementary attempt at
        measurement with less than satisfactory results.

2.41   Kohn, Hans, The Twentieth Century. New York, Macmillan,
        1949; especially, "Nationalism and the Open Society," pp. 19-31.

2.42   - - - World Order in Historical Perspective. Cambridge,

Harvard University Press, 1941.

2.43   - - - "Coalesce or Collide; Cultural Contact Engendered and Intensified Conflict between Nationalities," American Scholar, Vol. 9, No. 3, July 1940, pp. 261-273. Discussion Vol. 9, No. 4 Oct. 1940, pp. 505-507.

2.44   - - - "Nationalism," in Frank P. Davidson, Ed., Before America Decides, Cambridge, Harvard University Press, 1938, pp. 13-26.

2.45   - - - "The Nature of Nationalism," American Political Science Review, Vol. 33, Dec. 1939, pp. 101-121.

2.46   - - - "Twilight of Nationalism?" American Scholar, Vol. 6, No. 3, 1937, pp. 259-270.

2.47   Lampe, J., "Von der Völkischen zur Übervölkischen Ordnung, Internationale Arbeitsgemeinschaft der Nationalisten," Deutsche Rundschau, Vol. 244, Aug. 1935, pp. 143-147.

2.48   Lewis, W., "Nationalism," Bookman, Vol. 86, Sept. 1934, pp. 276-278.

2.49   Lot, F., "Qu'est-ce qu'une Nation?" Mercure de France, Vol. 306, May 1949, pp. 29-46.

2.50   Macartney, C. A., National States and National Minorities. London, H. Milford, Oxford University Press, 1934. P. Contains many data favoring the position of the Hungarian government between the wars.

2.51   - - - "War and the Small Nations," Fortnightly, Vol. 152 (new series Vol. 146), Oct. 1939, pp. 371-381.

2.52   Mander, L. A., "Nationalism: Ascendent or in Decline," Institute of World Affairs, Proceedings, Vol. 12, 1934, pp. 180-187.

2.53   Meinecke, Friedrich, Weltbuergertum und Nationalstaat, 7th Ed. Munich and Berlin, 1928 (Oldenbourg Verlag). P.

2.54   Oakley, Hilda D., "Nationalism and Civilization," Contemporary Review, Vol. 166, August 1944, pp. 95-99.

2.55   O'Toole, G. B., Race: Nation: Person. New York, Barnes and Noble, 1944. A sumposium of Roman Catholic writers.

2.56   Rocker, Rudolph, Nationalism and Culture, trans. Ray E. Chase. New York, Covici-Friede, 1937.

2.57   Rohrbach, P., "Nationale Parolen und Ideologien," Westermanns Monatshefte, Vol. 160, May 1936, pp. 222-224.

2.58   Roucek, J. S., Ed., "Nationalistic Ideology and Goals," Annals of the American Academy of Political and Social Science, Vol. 232, March 1944, pp. 25-115.

2.59   Stalin, Iosif V., Marxism and the National Question. New York,

International Publishers, 1942. The standard source for this point of view.

2.60   Stengel von Rutkowski, Lother, Was ist ein Volk? Der biolog-ische Volksbegriff. Erfurt, Verlag Kurt Stenger, 1943. A Nazi writer wrestles with the difficulties of the Nazi terminology.

2.61   Strasser, Josef, Der Arbeiter und die Nation, 2nd Ed. Reichen-berg, Runge, 1912. A Sudeten German critic of Bauer, and a source of some of Stalin's arguments.

2.62   Sturzo, Luigi, Nationalism and Internationalism. New York, Roy Publishers, 1946. The work of an outstanding Catholic sociologist and former leader of the Italian Popular Party.

2.63   Sulzbach, Walter, National Consciousness. Washington, D. C., American Council on Public Affairs, 1943. Written from the point of view of classical liberalism, the work stresses the non-economic and irrational aspects of national sentiment.

2.64   - - - "The New Nationalism (Gives the State First Place and the Individual Second)," South Atlantic Quarterly, Vol. 51, Oct. 1952, pp. 483-492.

2.65   Weill, Georges, Race et Nation, Collection Descartes: pour la verité. Paris, Albin Michel, 1939.

2.66   Werlin, J. S., "The Pathology of Hyper-Nationalism," South Western Social Science Quarterly, Vol. 20, Dec. 1939, pp. 300-311.

2.67   Winternitz, J., Marxism and Nationality. London, Lawrence and Wishart, Ltd., 1944.

2.68   Zimmern, Sir Alfred E., Modern Political Doctrines. London, New York, etc., Oxford University Press, 1939. Contains a section on nationalism with useful selections from Herder, Renan, J. S. Mill, Sun Yat Sen and others.

2.69   Zipf, George K., National Unity and Disunity: The Nation as a Bio-Social Organism. Bloomington, Ind., The Principia Press, Inc., 1944. Combines interesting mathematical methods with extreme naiveté in its political assumptions.

3.   POLITICAL SCIENCE

3.1   Almond, Gabriel H., The American People and Foreign Policy.
        New York, Harcourt Brace, 1950. Discusses U. S. foreign
        policy since the 1930's in connection with the "American
        National Character" using many quantitative results of Public
        Opinion polls.

3.2   - - - "Politics Science and Ethics," American Political Science
        Review, Vol. 40, No. 2, April 1946, pp. 283-293.

3.3   Anderson, H. F., "Sovereign Rights," Hibbert Journal, Vol. 38,
        Oct. 1939, pp. 24-32.

3.4   Arendt, Hannah, "Imperialism,Nationalism, Chauvinism," Review
        of Politics, Vol. 7, Oct. 1945, pp. 441-463.

3.5   Beaconsfield, Benjamin Disraeli, Earl of; Works, Earl's Ed.,
        16 vols. New York, Dunne, 1904.

3.6   Beer, Samuel H., The City of Reason. Cambridge, Harvard
        University Press, 194 . Stresses creative and combinatorial
        aspects of political thought in connection with the ideas of
        A. N. Whitehead.

3.7   Borning, Bernard C., "The Political Philosophy of Young Charles
        A. Beard," American Political Science Review, Vol. 43, No. 6,
        Dec. 1949. pp. 1165-1178.

3.7a   Bowie, Robert R., and Carl J. Friedrich, Studies in Federalism.
        Boston, Little Brown, 1954.

3.8   Brinton, Crane, From Many One: The Progress of Political
        Integration: The Problem of World Government. Cambridge,
        Harvard University Press, 1948. Well informed discussion.

3.9   Brodie, Bernard, Ed., The Absolute Weapon: Atomic Power
        and World Order. New York, Harcourt Brace, 1946. A signi-
        ficant extreme view of the impact of atomic weapons on national
        sovereignty. For an opposite opinion see P.M.S. Blackett, Fear,
        War and the Bomb. New York, Whittlesey House, 1949.

3.9a   Buchanan, William B., and Hadley Cantril, How Nations See Each
        Other: A Study in Public Opinion. Urbana, University of Illinois
        Press, 1953.

3.10   Burke, Edmund, Works, 4 vols., World's Classics Ed. London,
        Oxford University Press, 1906-1907.

3.11   Carleton, W. G., "Ideology or Balance of Power?" Yale Review,
        new series Vol. 36, No. 4, June 1947, pp. 590-602.

3.12   - - - "Is Communism Going National?" Virginia Quarterly
        Review, Vol. 25, No. 3, July 1949, pp. 321-334.

3.13   - - - "New Nationalism," Virginia Quarterly Review, Vol. 26,
        No. 3, July 1950, pp. 431-440.

3.14   Carr, Edward Hallett, Conditions of Peace. London, Macmillan,
        1942. Contains an interesting dicussion of the "they" rather
        than "we" attitude of people toward their national government
        in the 1930's.

3.15   - - - The Soviet Impact on the Western World. New York, Mac-
        millan, 1949. Discusses the reception of certain Soviet views
        and practices by anti-Communist governments which hastened
        "the disappearance of individualist values . . . and the substitu-
        tion for them of the social values of mass civilization"(p. 99).
        This thought is extended in the same author's The New Society.
        New York, Macmillan, 1951.

3.16   Catlin, G. E. G., The Story of the Political Philosophers. New
        York, Macmillan, 1939.

3.17   Center for International Studies, Massachusetts Institute of
        Technology, Research in International Communication: An
        Advisory Report of the Planning Committee. Cambridge, Mass.,
        1953.

3.17a   Claude, Inis L., Jr., National Minorities: An International
        Problem. Cambridge, Harvard University Press, 1955.

3.18   Cohen, Hyman Ezra, Recent Theories of Sovereignty. Chicago,
        University of Chicago Press, 1937.

3.19   Cole, G. D. H., Essays in Social Theory. London, Macmillan,
        1950; esp., "The Claims of Nationality," pp. 203-223. A
        theorist of the British Labor Party whose approach to Nation-
        alism has much in common with classic liberal views.

3.20   Cole, Kenneth C., "The Theory of the State as a Sovereign
        Juristic Person," American Political Science Review, Vol. 42,
        No. 1, Feb. 1948, pp. 16-31.

3.21   Corbett, P. E., "Future of Nationalism and the Nation-State,"
        Annals of the American Academy of Political and Social Science,
        Vol. 218, Nov. 1941, pp. 153-161.

3.22   Crossman, R. H. S., Government and the Governed: A History
        of Political Ideas and Political Practice. New York, Putnam's,
        1940. Stresses the importance of Tudor Absolutism as an engine
        of reform in forging the English national state. Should be con-
        trasted with the discussion of Tudor policy by K. Polanyi.

3.23   - - - "Nationalism: Enemy or Ally? Can Democracy Afford
        the Internationalist Fetish?" Commentary, Vol. 10, July 1950,
        pp. 1-6.

3.24   Cybichowsky, S., "National Sovereignty and International Cooper-
        ation," Annals of the American Academy of Political and Social
        Science, Vol. 186, July 1936, pp. 105-113.

3.25   Deutsch, Karl W., Political Community at the International Level
        Problems of Definition and Measurement. New York, Doubleday
        1954. (Random House, 1955).

3.26   - - - "Game Theory and Politics: Some Problems of Application,"
       Canadian Journal of Economics and Political Science, Vol. 20,
       No. 1, Feb. 1954, pp. 76-83.

3.27   - - - "Self-Referent Symbols and Self-Referent Communication
       Patterns: A Note on Some Pessimistic Theories of Politics,"
       in L. Bryson, et al. Eds., Symbols and Values: An Initial Study,
       New York, Harper, 1954, pp. 619-646.

3.28   Dolivet, L., "Educating Public Opinion for World Organization,"
       Annals of the American Academy of Political and Social Science,
       Vol. 222, July 1942, pp. 84-89.

3.29   Eagleton, C., "Excess of Self-Determination," Foreign Affairs,
       Vol. 31, July 1953, pp. 592-604.

3.30   - - - "Self-Determination in the United Nations," American
       Journal of International Law, Vol. 47, Jan. 1953, pp. 88-93.

3.31   Easton, David, The Political System: An Inquiry into the State
       of Political Science. New York, Knopf, 1953.

3.32   Ebenstein, Wilhelm, Man and the State: Modern Political Ideas.
       New York, Rinehart, 1948. "From Nationalism to World Order,"
       pp. 551-748. Bibliographical notes (on this topic) pp. 771-776.
       Contains excellent brief selections from Lord Acton, Mazzini,
       Masaryk, T. Herzl, and A. E. (George Russell).

3.33   Elliott, William Yandell, et al., The British Commonwealth at
       War. New York, Knopf, 1943.

3.34   - - - International Control in the Non-Ferrous Metals. New
       York, Macmillan, 1937. Examines the relation of international
       cartels and national rivalries in the vital field of raw materials,
       with a view to their wider political implication.

3.35   - - - The Pragmatic Revolt in Politics: Syndicalism, Fascism,
       and the Constitutional Republic. New York, Macmillan, 1928.
       A standard work of American political thought showing the
       effect of the Pragmatic frame of mind on both Democratic
       and Fascist ideas.

3.36   - - - and Neil A. McDonald, Western Political Heritage. New
       York, Prentice Hall, 1949.

3.37   - - - "The Pragmatic Revolt in Politics: Twenty Years in
       Retrospect," Review of Politics, Vol. 2, No. 1, Jan. 1940,
       pp. 1-11.

3.38   - - - "Prospects for Personal Freedom and Happiness for All
       Mankind," Annals of the American Academy of Political and
       Social Science, Vol. 268, March 1950, pp. 173-182.

3.39   Emerson, Rupert, "Point Four and Dependent Areas," Annals
       of the American Academy of Political and Social Science, Vol.
       268, March 1950, pp. 112-121. Stresses the possibility of gen-
       uine conflicts of interest: "The development of . . . secondary

industries in dependent areas may . . . do at least temporary
damage to the economy of the metropolitan country, but be of
central importance for the development of the colonial economy
. . . A concentration on the production of primary materials
for export is by no means necessarily an unmixed blessing for
colonial peoples."

3.40   Eulau, Heinz H. F., "The Depersonalization of the Concept of
Sovereignty," Journal of Politics, Vol. 4, No. 1, Feb. 1942,
pp. 3-19.

3.41   Fainsod Merle, International Socialism and the World War.
Cambridge, Harvard University Press, 1935.

3.42   Fox, William T. R., The Struggle for Atomic Control. New
York, Public Affairs Committee, Inc., 1947.

3.43   - - - The Super-Powers. New York, Harcourt Brace, 1944.

3.44   Friedmann, W., The Crisis of the National State. London, 1944.

3.45   - - - "Multi-National States," Fortnightly, Vol. 161 (new series
Vol. 155), May 1944, pp. 280-289.

3.46   - - - "Nazi and Soviet Nationalisms," Fortnightly, Vol. 170
(new series Vol. 164), Nov. 1948, pp. 289-294.

3.47   - - - "UNRRA and National Sovereignty," Fortnightly, Vol. 161
(new series Vol. 155), Jan. 1944, pp. 17-25.

3.48   Friedrich, Carl J., Constitutional Government and Politics,
2nd Ed. Boston, Ginn, 1950. A standard work in comparative
government.

3.49   - - - The New Belief in the Common Man. Boston, Little,
Brown, 1942. Enlarged Ed., Beacon Press, 1950.

3.50   - - - Ed., Totalitarianism. Cambridge, Harvard University
Press, 1954.

3.51   - - - "The Agricultural Basis of Emotional Nationalism,"
Public Opinion Quarterly, Vol. 1, No. 2, April 1937, pp. 50-61.

3.52   Frischauer, E. M., "Is Lasting Peace Possible?" South Atlantic
Quarterly, Vol. 43, Jan. 1944, pp. 11-21.

3.53   Ginsberg, Morris, "National Character," British Journal of
Psychology, Vol. 32, 1942, pp. 183-295.

3.54   Glasgow, G., "End of National Sovereignty," Contemporary
Review, Vol. 169, Jan. 1946, pp. 53-59.

3.55   Grace, Harry A. and Virginia Van Welzer, "Attitudes toward the
Universal Declaration of Human Rights: Perceptions of National
Actions," International Journal of Opinion and Attitude Research,
Winter, 1951-1952.

3.56   Guerard, A., "Culture and Territory: Fallacy of the National

State," Antioch Review, Vol. 1, June 1941, pp. 203-215.

3.57　Hobbes, Thomas, Leviathan, M. Oakeshott, Ed. Oxford B. Blackwell, 1946.

3.58　Hutton, David G., Survey after Munich. Boston, Little Brown, 1939.

3.59　Innis, H. A., "Geography and Nationalism," Geographical Review. Vol. 35, April 1945, pp. 301-311.

3.60　Isaacs, H. R., "Blind Alley of Totalitarianism," (excerpt) Pacific Spectator, Vol. 5, No. 4, 1951, pp. 382-396.

3.61　- - - "Political and Psychological Context of Point Four," Annals of the American Academy of Political and Social Science, Vol. 270, July 1950, pp. 51-58.

3.62　Jaeger, H., "Missbrauchte Kolonialvolker," Deutsche Rundschau, Vol. 78, Jan. 1952, pp. 15-18.

3.63　Jouvenel, Bertrand de., Power: Its Nature and the History of Its Growth. New York, Viking, 1949.

3.64　Katz, D., D. Cartwright, S. Elderveld and A. M. Lee, Edts., Public Opinion and Propaganda. New York, Dryden Press, 1954.

3.65　Kennan, George F., American Diplomacy, 1900-1950. Chicago, University of Chicago Press, 1951.

3.66　Laski, Harold J., The Foundations of Sovereignty and Other Essays. New Haven, Yale University Press, 1934.

3.67　- - - A Grammar of Politics, 2nd Ed. New Haven, Yale University Press, 1931.

3.68　- - - Liberty in the Modern State, new Ed. London, Allen and Unwin, 1948.

3.69　- - - The Rise of Liberalism: The Philosophy of a Civilization. New York, Harper, 1936.

3.70　- - - The State in Theory and Practice. New York, Viking, 1938.

3.71　Lasswell, Harold D., The Analysis of Political Behavior: An Empirical Approach. New York, Oxford University Press, 1949.

3.72　- - - National Security and Individual Freedom. New York, McGraw Hill, 1950.

3.73　- - - Politics: Who Gets What, When, How. New York, McGraw Hill, 1936. A standard work in its own way for the "tough minded" approach of the 1930's.

3.74　- - - Power and Personality. New York, Norton, 1943.

3.75　- - - Psychopathology and Politics. Chicago, University of Chicago Press, 1934. A pioneering study on the interplay of personality types, political movements, and crisis situations.

18

3.76   - - - World Politics and Personal Insecurity. New York, Whittlesey House, McGraw Hill, 1935.

3.77   - - - The World Revolution of Our Time: A Framework for Basic Policy Research. Stanford, Cal., Stanford University Press, 1951.

3.78   - - - , et al, Language of Politics: Studies in Quantitative Semantics. New York, G. W. Stewart, 1949.

3.79   - - - and Dorothy Blumenstock, World Revolutionary Propaganda: A Chicago Study. New York, Knopf, 1939. A study of communist propaganda in Chicago, concluding that the most effective antidote against it in practice had been the appeal to parochial and nationalistic sentiments.

3.80   - - - and H. Kaplan, Power and Society: A Framework for Political Inquiry. New Haven, Yale University Press, 1950.

3.81   - - - , Daniel Lerner and Ithiel Pool, The Comparative Study of Symbols. Stanford, Cal., Stanford University Press, 1952.

3.82   - - - , Daniel Lerner and Easton C. Rothwell, The Comparative Study of Elites and Introduction and Bibliography. Stanford, Cal., Stanford University Press, 1952.

3.83   - - - "Relation of Skill Politics to Class Politics and National Politics," Chinese Social and Political Science Review, Vol. 21, Oct. 1937, pp. 298-313.

3.84   Leighton, Alexander H., The Governing of Men: General Principles and Recommendations Based on Experience at a Japanese Relocation Camp. Princeton, Princeton University Press, 1946. An outstanding example of the successful application of psychiatric and anthropological skills to a political problem.

3.85   - - - Human Relations in a Changing World: Observations on the Use of the Social Sciences. New York, Dutton, 1949. Discusses the relation of the scientists's foresight to the administrator's power. It concludes that usually administrators turn to social scientists "as a drunk turns to a lamppost; for support rather than illumination." This is illustrated by an account of the ignoring of the reports of the Foreign Morale Analysis Division on Japanese readiness to surrender by the administrators who made the decision to drop the atom bomb on Hiroshima.

3.86   Lenin, V. I., State and Revolution. New York, International Publishers, 1932.

3.87   Lerner, Max, "The War as Revolution," Nation. Vol. 151, July 27, 1940, pp. 68-71.

3.88   Lindsay, A. D., Karl Marx ' Capital': An Introductory Essay. London, Oxford University Press, H. Milford, 1931.

3.89   - - - The Modern Democratic State. New York, Oxford

University Press, 1947. A discussion of the modern welfare
state combining much of both the liberal and the laboristic
traditions of Great Britain.

3.90 Lowenthal, Leo and Norbert Guterman, Prophets of Deceit: A
Study of the Techniques of the American Agitator. New York,
Harper, 1949.

3.91 MacDonald, Malcolm H., Marx, Engels and the National Questions.
Thesis Ph.D., Harvard University, 1939, unpublished.

3.92 Macridis, R. C., et al., "Research in Comparative Politics,"
American Political Science Review, Vol. 47, No. 3, Sept. 1953,
pp. 641-675.

3.93 Maritain, Jacques, The Person and the Common Good. New
York, Scribners, 1947. A concise but outstnading presentation
of the Thomistic distinction between individuality and personality
and of its modern political and social implication.

3.94 - - - Man and the State. Chicago, University of Chicago Press,
1951.

3.95 - - - "The Concept of Sovereignty," American Political Science
Review, Vol. 44, No. 2, June 1950, pp. 343-347.

3.96 - - - "The End of Machiavellianism," Review of Politics, Vol. 4,
No. 1, Jan. 1942, pp. 1-33. A fundamental attack on the Machia-
vellian tradition and the Neo-Machiavellian attempts to revive it.

3.97 Marriott, J. A. R., "Nationalism and Federalism," Quarterly
Review, Vol. 274, April 1940, pp. 325-343.

3.98 - - - "Problem of the Small State," Fortnightly, Vol. 157
(new series Vol.151), Feb. 1942, pp. 132-138.

3.99 Mathews, Donald R., The Social Background of Political Decision
Makers. New York, Doubleday, 1954.

3.100 McCoy, Charles N. R., "The Place of Machiavelli in the History
of Political Thought," American Political Science Review,
Vol. 37, No. 4, Aug. 1943, pp. 626-641.

3.101 McElroy, R., "International Law's Greatest Need," American
Journal of International Law, Vol. 37, Jan. 1943, pp. 117-120.

3.102 McGovern, William M., From Luther to Hitler. The History of
Fascist-Nazi Political Philosophy. Boston, Houghton Mifflin,
1941. Attempts to link the fascist and Nazi traditions not merely
to Nietzche and Pareto, but also to Immanuel Kant.

3.103 MacIver, Robert M., The More Perfect Union: A Program for
the Control of Inter-Group Discrimination in the United States.
New York, Macmillan, 1948.

3.104 - - - The Web of Government. New York, Macmillan, 1947.

3.105   Menczer, B., "Survival of Nations," Twentieth Century, Vol. 138, Nov. 1945, pp. 219-222.

3.106   Merriam, Charles E., The Making of Citizens. A Comparative Study of the Methods of Civic Training. Chicago, University of Chicago Press, 1931. P. The summary of a many-volume survey of methods of national and civic indoctrination in various countries.

3.107   - - - Systematic Politics. Chicago, University of Chicago Press, 1945.

3.108   - - - "Physics and Politics," American Political Science Review, Vol. 40, No. 3, June 1946, pp. 445-457.

3.109   Meyer, Cord, Peace or Anarchy. Boston, Little Brown, 1947.

3.110   Mitrany, D., "International Consequences of National Planning," Yale Review (new series), Vol. 37, No. 1, Sept. 1947, pp. 18-31.

3.111   Moos, Malcolm, "Don Luigi Sturzo - Christian Democrat," American Political Science Review, Vol. 39, No. 2, April 1945, pp. 269-292.

3.112   Morgenthau, Hans, In Defense of the National Interest. New York, Knopf, 1951.

3.113   - - - Politics Among Nations. New York, Knopf, 1948, 2nd ed. 1953.

3.114   - - - Scientific Man Vs. Power Politics. Chicago, University of Chicago Press, 1946.

3.115   - - - and Kenneth W. Thompson, Principles and Problems of International Politics: Selected Readings. New York Knopf, 1950.

3.116   - - - "Conduct of American Foreign Policy," Parliamentary Affairs, Vol. 3, 1949, pp. 1-16.

3.117   - - - "The Conquest of the United States by Germany," Bulletin of the Atomic Scientists, Vol. 6, 1950, pp. 21-26.

3.118   - - - "The National Interest Versus Moral Abstractions," American Political Science Review, December 1950. "A foreign policy derived from the national interest is in fact morally superior to a foreign policy inspired by universal moral principles."

3.119   - - - "Twilight of International Morality," Ethics, Vol. 58, Jan. 1948, pp. 79-99.

3.120   - - - "World Politics in the Mid-Twentieth Century," Review of Politics, Vol. 10, April 1948, pp. 154-173.

3.121   Mosca, Gaetano, The Ruling Class. New York, McGraw-Hill, 1939.

3.122   Neumann, Franz, "Approaches to the Study of Political Power," Political Science Quarterly, Vol. 65, No. 2, June, 1950.

3.123   Neumann, Sigmund, "The International Civil War," World Politics, Vol. 1, 1948, pp. 333-350.

3.123a   Northrop, F. S. C., European Union and United States Foreign Policy: A Study in Sociological Jurisprudence. New York, Macmillan, 1954.

3.124   Ogburn, William F., ed., Technology and International Relations. Chicago, University of Chicago Press, 1949.

3.125   Orwell, George, 1984. New York, Harcourt Brace, 1949.

3.126   Padelford, Norman, J., Contemporary International Relations: Readings, 1950-1951. Cambridge, Harvard University Press, 1951 (esp. Chap. III).

3.127   - - - International Relations: Fundamentals and Problems. Cambridge, Mass. Institute of Technology, 1950 (esp. Chaps. V-VI).

3.128   Pareto, Vilfredo, The Mind and Society, 4 vols. New York, Harcourt Brace, 1942.

3.129   Pool, Ithiel and others, The ' Prestige Papers ': A Survey of Their Editorials. Stanford, Cal., Stanford University Press, 1952.

3.130   - - - Symbols of Democracy. Stanford, Cal., Stanford University Press, 1952.

3.131   - - - Symbols of Internationalism. Stanford, Cal., Stanford University Press, 1951.

3.132   Potter, Pitman, B., "Universalism Vs. Regionalism in International Organization," American Political Science Review, Vol. 37, No. 5, Oct. 1943, pp. 850-861.

3.133   Rappard, W. E., "Relation of the Individual to the State," Annals of the American Academy of Political and Social Science, Vol. 189, Jan. 1937, pp. 215-218.

3.134   Recasens-Siches, Luis, Vida Human, Sociedad y Derecho: Fundamentos de la Filosofia del Derecho, 2nd Ed. Mexico, Fondo de Cultura Economica, 1945.

3.135   - - - "Human Life, Society and Law: Fundamentals of the Philosophy of the Law," in Latin American Legal Philosophy, Cambridge, Harvard University Press, 1948, pp. 1-341.

3.136   Reves, Emery, The Anatomy of Peace. New York, Harper, 1946. Asserts that "unintegrated sovereignties" as such must produce wars, and pleads for almost immediate world government.

3.137   Richards, Ivor A., Nations and Peace. New York, Simon and Schuster, 1947.

3.138   Ruchames, Louis, Race, Jobs and Politics. New York, Columbia University Press, 1953.

3.139   Russell, Bertrand, Authority and the Individual. New York, Simon and Schuster, 1948.

3.140   - - - Power: A New Social Analysis. New York, Norton, 1938.

3.141   - - - "Revolt against Reason," Political Quarterly, Vol. 6, Jan. 1935, pp. 1-19.

3.142   Sabine, G. H., A History of Political Theory, 2nd Ed. New York, Holt, 1950.

3.143   Samhaber, E., "Von Weltpolitischen Entscheidungen," Deutsche Rundschau, Vol. 249, Nov. 1936, pp. 97-103.

3.143a Schiffer, Walter, The Legal Community of Mankind. New York, Columbia University Press, 1954.

3.144   Schuman, Frederick L., The Commonwealth of Man. New York, Knopf, 1952.

3.145   - - - International Politics: The Western State System in Transition, 5th Ed. New York, McGraw-Hill, 1953.

3.146   - - - "International Ideals and the National Interest," The Annals of the American Academy of Political and Social Science, Philadelphia, March 1952, pp. 27-36.

3.147   Schwarzenberger, G., Power Politics: A Study of International Society. Frederick A. Praeger, New York, 1951.

3.148   Simonds, Frank H., The Great Powers in World Politics: International Relations and Economic Nationalism. New York, Cincinnati, etc., American Book Co., 1937.

3.149   Snell, L. W., "The Growth of National Self-Sufficiency: What Next?" Hibbert Journal, Vol. 33, Jan. 1935, pp. 263-276.

3.150   Spahr, Margaret, "Sovereignty under Law: A Possible Redefinition of Sovereignty in the Light of Locke's Theory of Liberty." American Political Science Review, Vol. 39, No. 2, April 1945, pp. 350-355.

3.151   Spengler, Oswald, The Decline of the West. New York, Knopf, 1939.

3.152   - - - Gedanken. Munich, H. C. Beck, 1941.

3.153   Stone, Julius, The Province and Function of Law. London, Stevens 1947; Sydney, Australia, Associated General Publications, 1946. (esp. pp. 421-448, "Law and National Development," and pp. 442-444, "The Main Caveats on the Volksgeist Doctrine.")

3.154   Streit, Clarence K., Union Now: A Proposal for a Federal Union of the Democracies of the North Atlantic. New York, Harper, 1939; postwar ed., (revised), 1949.

3.155   Thomas, N., "National Interests and World Peace," Annals of the American Academy of Political and Social Science, Vol. 288, July 1952, pp. 72-76.

3.156   Truman, David B., The Governmental Process: Political
        Interests and Public Opinion. New York, Knopf, 1951.

3.157   United Nations Department of Social Affairs, A Study of State-
        lessness. Lake Success, New York, 1949, E/1112, 1 February
        1949, 3/1112/Add. 1, 19 May 1949; Sales No.: 1949, XIV, 2.

3.158   United Nations General Assembly, Fourth Committee, "Factors
        Adopted for Deciding Identity of Territories," United Nations
        Bulletin, Vol. 15, Oct. 15, 1953, pp. 339-344.

3.159   Utley, T. E., "Conservatism, Nations and Groups," National
        Review, Vol. 130, April 1948, pp. 287-291.

3.160   Vielvölkerheere und Koalitionskriege. Auslandsforschung:
        Schriftenreihe der Auslandswissenschaftlichen Gesellschaft;
        Heft 1, Darmstadt, C. W. Leske, 1952. Includes: Gunther Ipsen,
        "Das Heer der Österreichisch-Ungarischen Monarchie,"
        pp. 40-47; Nicolae Alexandru, "Die Rumänen in der Oster-
        reichischen Armee," pp. 48-52.

3.161   Wallas, Graham, Human Nature in Politics. New York, Knopf,
        1941.

3.162   Wambaugh, Sarah, Plebiscites Since the World War, 2 vols.
        Washington, Carnegie Endowment for International Peace, 1933.

3.163   White L. and R. D. Leigh, Peoples Speaking to Peoples. Chicago,
        University of Chicago Press, 1946.

3.164   Wight, Martin, Power Politics: An Introductory Essay. New
        York, Royal Institute of International Affairs, 1954.

3.165   Woodruff, D., "Strong Nations or Strong States?" International
        Affairs, Vol. 23, Jan. 1947, pp. 61-71.

4.   THEORY OF COMMUNICATION

4.1   Ashby, W. Ross, Design for a Brain. London, Chapman and
        Hall, 1952.

4.2   Berkeley, E. C., Giant Brains. New York, John Wiley and Sons,
        Inc., 1949.

4.3   Cannon, W., The Wisdom of the Body. New York, Norton, 1923.

4.4   Churchman, C. W. and R. L. Ackoff, "Purposive Behaviour and
        Cybernetics," Social Forces, Vol. 29, No. 1, Oct. 1950, pp. 32-39.

4.5   Deutsch, Karl W., "Higher Education and the Unity of Knowledge,"
        Goals for American Education: Ninth Symposium of the Confer-
        ence on Science, Philosophy, and Religion, New York, Harper,
        1950, pp. 55-139; esp. Part VI, Sect. 2, pp. 102-136.

4.6   - - - "Innovation, Entrepreneurship, and the Learning Process,"
        in Change and the Entrepreneur, Cambridge, Harvard Univer-
        sity Press, 1949.

4.7   - - - "Mechanism, Organism, and Society," Philosophy of
        Science, Vol. 18, No. 3, July 1951, pp. 230-252.

4.8   "Mechanism, Teleology and Mind: The Theory of Communica-
        tions and Some Problems in Philosophy and Social Science,"
        Philosophy and Phenomenological Research, Vol. 12, No. 2,
        Dec. 1951, pp. 185-223.

4.9   Fano, R. M., "The Information Theory Point of View in Speech
        Communication," Journal of the Acoustical Society of America,
        Nov. 1950.

4.10   - - - The Transmission of Information. M.I.T. Research
        Laboratory of Electronics, Technical Report No. 65.

4.11   - - - The Transmission of Information, Part II, M.I.T. Research
        Laboratory of Electronics, Technical Report No. 149.

4.12   Festinger, L., K. Back, S. Schachter, H. H. Kelley and J. Thibaut,
        Theory and Experiment in Social Communication. Ann Arbor,
        Institute for Social Research, University of Michigan, 1950.

4.13   Frank, L. K., Foreword to "Teleogical Mechanisms," Annals of
        the New York Academy of Sciences, Vol. 50, Oct. 1948, pp. 189-
        196.

4.14   Hebb, D. O., The Organization of Behavior. New York, Wiley,
        1949.

4.15   Hertz, D. and R. T. Livingston," The Engineer and Organization
        and Management," Human Relations, Spring 1951.

4.16   Massachusetts Institute of Technology, A Bibliography of Cyber-
        netics. Compiled by the Group Networks Laboratory and by the
        Industrial Relations Laboratory, 1951. Multigraphed.

4.17   McCulloch, Warren, S., "Finality and Form in Nervous Activity," Fifteenth James Arthur Lecture, American Museum of Natural History, New York, May 2, 1946. Multigraphed.

4.18   - - - and W. Pitts, "A Logical Calculus of the Ideas Immanent in Nervous Activity," Bulletin of Mathematical Biophysics, V, 1943, pp. 115-133.

4.19   - - - "A Recapitulation of the Theory, with a Forecast of Several Extensions," in Teleological Mechanisms; Annals of the New York Academy of Sciences, Vol. 50, Article 4, Oct. 1948, pp. 247-258.

4.20   Morris, C. W., Signs, Language and Behavior. New York, Prentice-Hall, 1946.

4.21   Neiman, Peter B., The Operational Significance of Recognition. B. S. Thesis, Course IX, M.I.T., 1949, Unpublished.

4.22   Northrop, F. C. S., "The Neurological and Behavioristic Basis of the Ordering of Society by Means of Ideas," Science, Vol. 107, No. 2782, April 23, 1948.

4.23   Rosenblueth, A., and N. Wiener, "Purposeful and Non-purposeful Behavior," Philosophy of Science, Vol. 17, Oct. 1950.

4.24   - - - "The Role of Models in Science, " Philosophy of Science, Vol. XII, pp. 316-322, (1945).

4.25   - - - , - - - and Bigelow, Jr., "Behavior, Purpose, and Teleology," Philosophy of Science, Vol. X, No. 1, Jan. 1943, pp. 18-24.

4.26   Shannon, C. E. and W. Weaver, The Mathematical Theory of Communication. Urbana, University of Illinois Press, 1949.

4.27   Shannon, C. E., "A Chess Playing Machine," Scientific American, Vol. 182, No. 2, Feb. 1950.

4.28   - - - "Memory Requirements in a Telephone Exchange," Bell System Technical Journal, July 1950.

4.29   - - - Prediction and Entropy of Printed English," Bell System Technical Journal, Vol. 30:1, Jan. 1951.

4.30   - - - "Programming a Computer for Playing Chess," Philosophical Magazine, Series 7, Vol. XLI, March 1950, pp. 256-275.

4.31   von Foerster, Heinz, Margaret Mead and Hans Lukas Teuber, eds., Cybernetics: Circular Causal and Feedback Mechanisms in Biological and Social Sciences. Transactions of the Eighth Conference, March 15-16, 1951, New York, Josiah Macy, Jr. Foundation, 565 Park Avenue.

4.32   Wiener, Norbert, Cybernetics. New York, John Wiley & Sons, Inc.; Cambridge, Massachusetts Institute of Technology Press, 1948.

4.33   - - - Extrapolation, Interpolation, and Smoothing of Stationary Time Series. New York, John Wiley & Sons, Inc.; Cambridge,

Massachusetts Institute of Technology Press, 1949.

4.34   - - - The Human Use of Human Beings: Cybernetics and Society. Boston, Houghton Mifflin, 1950; New York, Double-day Archer Books, 1954.

4.35   - - - "Speech, Language, and Learning," Journal of the Acoustical Society of America, Nov. 1950.

4.36   Yule, G. U., The Statistical Study of Literary Vocabulary. London, Cambridge, 1944.

4.37   Zipf, G. K., "Some Determinants of the Circulation of Information," American Journal of Psychology, Vol. 59, 1946, pp. 401-421.

5.   CULTURAL ANTHROPOLOGY, SOCIOLOGY AND SOCIAL PSYCHOLOGY

5.1   Abel, T. M., "The Rorschach Test in the Study of Culture," Rorschach Research, Exchange and Journal of Projective Techniques, Vol. 12, 1948, pp. 70-93.

5.2   Ackerman, N. W. and M. Jahoda, Antisemitism and Emotional Disorder: A Psychoanalytic Interpretation. New York, Harper, 1950.

5.3   Adorno, T. W., E. Frenkel-Brunswick, D. J. Levinson and R. N. Sanford, The Authoritarian Personality. New York, Harper, 1950.

       5.3 a   Allport, Gordon, W., The Nature of Prejudice. Cambridge, Addison-Wesley, 1954.

5.4   - - - Personality: A Psychological Interpretation. New York, Holt, 1937.

5.5   - - - "Prejudices: A Problem of Psychological and Social Causation," Social Issues, Supplement Series No. 4, 1950.

5.6   - - - "The Role of Expectancy," in H. Cantril Ed., Tensions that Cause Wars, Urbana, University of Illinois Press, 1940, pp. 43-78.

5.6a   Anikeeff, Alexis M., Dynamics of Intersectional Tension. Business Research Station Special Study Series Bulletin No. 7, 1952.

5.7   Appel, K. E., "Nationalism and Sovereignty: A Psychiatric View," Journal of Abnormal Psychology, Vol. 40, Oct. 1945, pp. 335-362.

5.8   Bartlett, F. C., Remembering. Cambridge, Cambridge, University Press, 1932.

5.9   Bateson, Gregory, "Atoms, Nations, and Culture," The International House Quarterly, Vol. II, No. 2, Spring, 1947, pp. 47-50.

5.10   - - - "Morale and National Character," in Goodwin Watson Ed., Civilian Morale: Second Yearbook of the Society for the Psychological Study of Social Issues, Boston, Houghton Mifflin, 1942, pp. 71-91.

5.11   - - - "The Patterning of an Armaments Race," Part I, "An Anthropological Approach"; Part II, "An Analysis of Nationalism." Bulletin of Atomic Scientists, Vol. 2, No. 5 and 6, 1946, pp. 10-11; No. 7 and 8, pp. 26-28.

5.12   Bell, John Elderkin, Projective Techniques: A Dynamic Approach to the Study of the Personality. New York, Longmans, Green, 1948.

5.13   Benedict, Ruth, Patterns of Culture. New York, Pelican-Mentor, 1947.

5.14   Berelson, B. and P. Salter, "Majority and Minority Americans:

An Analysis of Magazine Fiction," Public Opinion Quarterly Vol. 10, 1946, pp. 168-190.

5.15   Berkson, Isaac, Theories of Americanization. New York, Teachers College Publications, Columbia University, 1920.

5.16   Bogardus, E. S., Immigration and Race Attitudes. New York, Heath, 1928.

5.17   - - - "Measuring Social Distances," Journal of Applied Sociology, Vol. 9, 1925, pp. 299-308.

5.18   - - - "A Social Distance Scale," Sociology and Social Research, Vol. 17, 1933, pp. 265-271.

5.19   Brann, H. W., "Is the Complete Disappearance of Racial and National Prejudice Realizable?" Southwestern Social Science Quarterly, Vol. 26, June 1945, pp. 76-85.

5.20   Campbell, Angus, "Factors Associated with Attitudes toward Jews," in T. M. Newcomb and E. L. Hartley Ed., Readings in Social Psychology, New York, Holt, 1947, pp. 518-527.

5.21   - - - A Survey Research Approach to National Character. Ann Arbor, Institute for Social Research, University of Michigan, 1949. Multigraphed.

5.22   Canada-United States Committee on Education, A Study of National History Textbooks Used in Schoolssof Canada and the United States. Washington, D. C., 1947.

5.23   Cantril, Hadley, Ed., Tensions that Cause Wars: Common Statement and Individual Papers by a Group of Social Scientists Brought Together by UNESCO. Urbana, University of Illinois Press, 1950.

5.24   Carter, H., "Recent American Studies in Attitudes Toward War: A Summary and Evaluation," American Sociological Review, Vol. 10, 1945, pp. 343-352.

5.25   Chapple, Eliot Dismore, and Carleton Stevens Coon, Principles of Anthropology. New York, Holt, 1942.

5.26   Chase, Stuart, The Proper Study of Mankind. New York, Harper, 1948.

5.27   Claparède, E., "Psychologie de la Comprehension Internationale," in H. Pieron and I. Meyerson Eds., Le Onzième Congrès International de Psychologie, Paris, Alcan, 1938.

5.28   Cottrell, W. F., "Cultural Growth of Internationalism," American Sociological Review, Vol. 10, Oct. 1945, pp. 586-595.

5.29   Crisswell, J. H., "The Measurement of Group Integration," Sociometry, Vol. 10, No. 3, 1947, pp. 259-267.

5.30   - - - "Racial Cleavages in Negro-White Groups," Sociometry, Vol. 1, 1937, pp. 87-89.

5.31   - - - "Sociometric Methods of Measuring Group Preferences,"
        Sociometry, Vol. 6, No. 4, 1943, pp. 398-408.

5.32   Davie, Maurice R., World Immigration. New York, Macmillan,
        1943.

5.33   Dingwall, E. J., Racial Pride and Prejudice. London, Watts,
        1946.

5.34   Dollard, John, et al., Frustration and Aggression. New Haven,
        Yale University Press, 1939.

5.35   - - - The Plans of Men. New Haven, Yale University Press,
        1940.

5.36   Doob, Leonard W., Public Opinion and Propaganda. New York,
        Holt, 1948.

5.37   DuBois, Cora, et al., The People of Alor. Minneapolis, Univer-
        sity of Minnesota Press, 1944.

5.38   Duncan, G. H., Immigration and Assimilation. Boston, Heath,
        1933.

5.39   Edwards, A. L. and K. D. Kenney, "A Comparison of the Thur-
        stone and Likert Techniques of Attitude Scale Construction,"
        Journal of Applied Psychology, Vol. 30, 1946, pp. 72-83.

5.40   Eysenck, J. J. and S. Crown, "National Stereotypes: An Experi-
        mental and Methodological Study," International Journal of
        Opinions and Attitude Research, Vol. 2, 1948, pp. 26-39.

5.41   Fairchild, Henry Pratt, Immigration. New York, Macmillan,
        1925.

5.42   - - - Immigration Backgrounds. New York, Wiley, 1927.

5.43   - - - Dictionary of Sociology. New York, Philosophical
        Library, 1944.

5.44   Fellner, E., "Psychology of Nationalism," Hibbert Journal,
        Vol. 47, April 1949, pp. 266-271.

5.45   Ferguson, L. W., "Isolation and Measurement of Nationalism,"
        Journal of Social Psychology, Vol. 16, Nov. 1942, pp. 215-228.

5.46   Fife, R. H., "Nationalism and Scholarship," Proceedings of
        the Modern Language Association, Vol. 59, Supplement, 1944,
        pp. 1282-1294.

5.47   Firth, Raymond, Elements of Social Organization. London,
        Watts, 1951; especially "Social Change in Peasant Com-
        munities," pp. 80-121.

5.48   Francis, E. K., "Nature of the Ethnic Group," American
        Journal of Sociology, Vol. 52, March 1947, pp. 393-400.

5.49   Frenkel- Brunswick, E., "Intolerance of Ambiguity as an
        Emotional and Cognitive Personality Variable," Journal of

Personality, Vol. 18, 1949, pp. 108-143.

5.50 - - - "Mechanisms of Self-Deception," Journal of Social
Psychology, Vol. 10, 1939, pp. 409-420.

5.51 Freud, Siegmund, Civilization and Its Discontents. London,
1930.

5.52 Fromm, Erich, Escape from Freedom. New York, Farrar and
Rinehart, 1941.

5.53 - - - Man for Himself: An Inquiry into the Psychology of Ethics.
New York, Rinehart, 1947; especially "The Marketing Orienta-
tion," pp. 67-82.

5.54 - - - Psychoanalysis and Religion. New Haven, Yale University
Press, 1950.

5.55 Fyfe, H., "Illusion of National Character," Political Quarterly,
Vol. 9, April 1938, pp. 254-270.

5.56 Gierlichs, Willy, "Zur Soziologie der 'Umvolkung' als Gegenwarts-
problem," Volksforschung, Vol. 3, No. 1 (Stuttgart, Enke Verlag),
May 1939, pp. 1-7.

5.57 Gillin, John, Ed., For a Science of Social Man: Convergences
in Anthropology, Psychology, and Sociology. New York, Macmillan, 1954.

5.58 Ginsberg, Morris, Reason and Unreason in Society. Cambridge,
Harvard University Press, 1948.

5.59 - - - "National Character," British Journal of Psychology,
Vol. 32, pp. 183-205.

5.60 Goode, William J. and P. K. Hatt, Methods of Social Research.
New York, McGraw-Hill, 1952.

5.60a Gorer, Geoffrey, "The Concept of National Character," Science
News, No. 18 (Harmondsworth, Middlesex, Penguin Books), 1950,
pp. 105-122.

5.61 Grodzins, Morton, "The Basis of National Loyalty," Bulletin
of the Atomic Scientists, Vol. 7, No. 12, Dec. 1951, pp. 356-362.

5.62 Guenther, Adolf, "Soziologie des Grenzvolkes erlaeutert an den
Alpenlaendern," in G. Salomon Ed., Jahrbuch füer Soziologie,
III, Karlsruhe, Braun, 1927, pp. 200-234.

5.63 Gundlach, Ralph H., "The Psychological Bases for Permanent
Peace," Journal of Social Psychology,Vol. 16, 1942, pp. 297-334.

5.64 Harper, H. R., What European and American Students Think on
International Problems. New York, Columbia University Press,
1931.

5.65 Hartley, E. L., Problems in Prejudice. New York, King's Crown,
1946.

5.66   Hellpach, Willy, Einführung in die Voelkerpsychologie, 2nd Revised Ed. Stuttgart, Ferdinand Enke Verlag, 1944.

5.67   Herskovits, Melville J., Acculturation. New York, Augustin, 1938.

5.68   - - - Man and His Works. New York, Knopf, 1948.

5.69   Hertz, Friederich O., "National Spirit and National Peculiarities," American Sociological Review, Vol. 26, 1934.

5.70   - - - "Nature of Nationalism," Social Forces, Vol. 19, March 1941, pp. 409-415.

5.71   Hovland, C. I., and R. R. Sears, "Minor Studies in Aggression: VI. Correlations of Lynchings with Economic Indices," Journal of Psychology, Vol. 9, 1940, pp. 301-310.

5.72   Ichheister, G., "Misunderstandings in International Relations," American Sociological Review, Vol. 16, June 1951, pp. 311-316.

5.73   - - - "Some Psychological Obstacles to an Understanding between the Nations; Some of the Socio-Psychological Forms of Unconscious Nationalism," Journal of Abnormal Psychology, Vol. 36, July 1941, pp. 428-432.

5.73a   Inkeles, Alex and Daniel J. Levinson, "National Character: The Study of Modal Personality and Socio-Cultural Systems," in G. Lindzey, ed., Handbook of Social Psychology, Cambridge, Addison-Wesley, Vol. 2, pp. 977-1020, Incl. Bibliography.

5.73b   Jacobson, Eugene and Stanley Schachter, "Cross-National Research: A Case Study," a special issue of Journal of Social Issues, Vol. 10, No. 4, 1954.

5.74   Jenkins, D., "Feedback and Group Self-Evaluation," Journal of Social Issues, Vol. 2, 1948, pp. 50-60.

5.75   Johnson, Charles S., "The Vanishing Mulatto: A Study in Personality and Culture Conflict," Opportunity, Oct. 1925, p. 291.

5.76   Kardiner, Abraham, The Individual and His Society, New York, Columbia University Press, 1939.

5.77   Klineberg, Otto, Social Psychology, New York, Holt, 1940.

5.78   Kluckhohn, Clyde, Mirror for Man: The Relation of Anthropology to Modern Life, New York, McGraw-Hill, 1949.

5.79   - - - and H. A. Murray, Eds., Personality in Nature, Society and Culture. New York, Knopf, 1948.

5.80   Krech, David and R. S. Crutchfield, Theory and Problems of Social Psychology. New York, McGraw-Hill, 1948.

5.81   Kroeber, A. L., Configurations of Culture Growth. Berkeley, University of California Press, 1944.

5.82   - - - "Configurations, Causes and St. Augustine," American Anthropologist, Vol. 53, No. 2, April-June 1951, pp. 279-284.

32

5.83   - - - , and J. Richardson, "Three Centuries of Women's Dress
        Fashions," Anthropological Records, Berkeley, 1940.

5.84   La Pierre, Richard T., Collective Behavior. New York, McGraw-
        Hill, 1938.

5.85   Lazarsfeld, Paul F., Radio and the Printed Page. New York,
        Duell, Sloan and Pearce, 1940.

5.86   - - - , B. Berelson and H. Gaudet, The People's Choice, 2nd Ed.
        New York, Columbia University Press, 1948.

5.87   - - - and F. N. Stanton, eds., Communications Research. New
        York, Harper, 1949.

5.88   - - - "Communication Research and the Social Psychologist,"
        in Wayne Dennis ed., Current Trends in Social Psychology,
        Pittsburgh, University of Pittsburgh Press, 1948.

5.89   - - - "Panel Studies," Public Opinion Quarterly, Vol. 4, 1940,
        pp. 122-128.

5.90   - - - and Genevieve Knupfer, "Communications Research and
        International Cooperation," in Ralph Linton ed., The Science
        of Man in the World Crisis, New York, Columbia University
        Press, 1945, pp. 465-495.

5.91   Lehmann, G., Das Kollektivbewusstsein, Systematische und
        historischkritische Vorstudien zur Soziologie, Berlin, Junker
        & Duennhaupt, 1928.

5.92   Levi-Strauss, Claude, "Language and the Analysis of Social
        Laws," American Anthropologist, Vol. 53, No. 2, April-June
        1951, pp. 155-163.

5.93   - - - Les Structures Elementaires de la Parenté. Paris, 1949.

5.94   Linton, Ralph, The Cultural Background of Personality. New
        York, Appleton-Century Co., 1945.

5.95   - - -, ed., The Science of Man in the World Crisis. New York
        Columbia University Press, 1945.

5.96   Lippitt, Ronald, Training in Community Relations. New York,
        Harper, 1949.

5.97   Locke, Alain LeRoy and Bernhard J. Stern, When Peoples Meet: A
        Study in Race and Culture Contacts, Revised Ed. New York,
        Hinds, Hayden and Eldredge, 1946.

5.98   Maier, N. R. F., Frustration: The Study of Behavior without a
        Goal. New York, McGraw-Hill, 1949.

5.99   Malinowski, Bronislaw, "Culture," in Encyclopedia of the Social
        Sciences, Vol. 2, New York, Macmillan, 1937, pp. 621 f.

5.100   - - - "Tribe-Nation and Tribe-State," in Freedom and Civiliza-
        tion, New York, Roy, 1944, pp. 252-263.

5.101 Mannheim, Karl, Diagnosis of Our Time. New York, Oxford University Press, 1944.

5.102 - - - Freedom, Power and Democratic Planning. New York, Oxford University Press, 1950.

5.103 - - - Ideology and Utopia. New York, Harcourt Brace, 1947. A major work by one of the peioneers in the field of "the sociology of knowledge."

5.104 - - - Man and Society in the Age of Reconstruction. New York, Harcourt Brace, 1948. Discusses the difficulties and opportunities for free government in the face of increasing needs for planning and increasing "fundamental democratisation," i.e. social and political activity by the masses of the population.

5.105 Martin, H., "Nationalism and Children's Literature," Library Quarterly, Vol. 6, 1936, pp. 405-418.

5.106 McGeoch, J. A., The Psychology of Human Learning. London, Longmans, 1942.

5.107 McGranahan, Donald G., "A Comparison of Social Attitudes among American and German Youth," Journal of Abnormal and Social Psychology, Vol. 41, 1946, pp. 245-257.

5.108 - - - and Ivor Wayne, "German and American Traits Reflected in Popular Drama," Human Relations, Vol. 1, 1948, pp. 429-455. See also item 5.126.

5.109 MacIver, Robert M., Discrimination and National Welfare, New York, Harper, 1949.

5.110 - - - Social Causation, Boston, Ginn, 1942.

5.111 - - - and C. H. Page, Society: An Introductory Analysis. New York, Rinehart, 1949.

5.112 Mead, Margaret and Frances Cooke Macgregor, Growth and Culture, a Photographic Study of Balinese Childhood. New York, Putnam, 1951.

5.113 - - - , ed., Cooperation and Competition among Primitive Peoples. New York, McGraw-Hill, 1937.

5.114 - - - "The Application of Anthropological Techniques to Cross-National Communication," Transactions, New York Academy of Sciences, Series II, Vol. 9, No. 4, Feb. 1947, pp. 133-152.

5.115 - - - "The Comparative Study of Cultures and the Purposive Cultivation of Democratic Values, 1941-1949," in L. Bryson Ed., Perspectives on a Troubled Decade: 1940-1950, New York, Harper, 1950, pp. 87-108.

5.116 - - - "People and Projects," Human Organization, Vol. 8, No. 1, Winter 1949.

5.117 - - - "Research in Contemporary Culture," in Groups, Leadership and Men, Carnegie Institute of Technology, Carnegie Press, Pittsburgh, 1951, pp. 106-118.

5.117a   - - - "The Swaddling Hypothesis: Its Reception," American Anthropologist, Vol. 56, No. 3, June 1954, pp. 395-409.

5.118   Meltzer, H., "The Development of Children's Nationality Preferences, Concepts and Attitudes," Journal of Psychology, Vol. 11, April 1941, pp. 343-358.

5.119   Merton, Robert K., Mass Persuasion: The Social Psychology of a War Bond Drive, New York, Harper, 1946.

5.120   - - - , P. S. West and Marie Jahoda, Patterns of Living: Explorations in the Sociology of Housing. New York, Harper, 1952.

5.121   - - -, Ailsa P. Gray, et al., eds., Reader in Bureaucracy. Glencoe, Ill., Free Press, 1952.

5.122   - - - and P. F. Lazarsfeld, eds., Continuities in Social Research. Glencoe, Ill., Free Press, 1950.

5.123   - - -,"Fact and Factitiousness in Ethnic Opinionnaires," American Sociological Review, Vol. 5, 1940, pp. 13-28.

5.124   Metraux, A., "Technical Assistance and Anthropology," American Anthropologist, Vol. 53, No. 3, July-Sept. 1951, pp. 419-420.

5.125   - - - "UNESCO and Anthropology," American Anthropologist, Vol. 53, No. 2, April-June 1951, pp. 294-300.

5.126   Miller, James Grier, ed., Experiments in Social Process: A Symposium on Social Psychology. New York, McGraw-Hill, 1950; especially Chapter 7: D. V. McGranahan and Ivor Wayne, "A Comparative Study of National Characteristics," pp. 99-146.

5.127   Moreno, J. L., Who Shall Survive? Foundation of Sociometry, Group Psychotherapy and Psychodrama, Revised Ed. New York, Beacon House, 1953.

5.128   Mowrer, O. H., Learning Theory and Personality Dynamics. New York, Ronald, 1950.

5.129   Mueller-Freinenfels, R., The Evolution of Modern Psychology. New Haven, Yale University Press, 1935.

5.130   Murdock, G. P., "Ethnocentrism," Encyclopedia of the Social Sciences, Vol. 5, New York, 1937, pp. 613.

5.131   - - - Social Structure. New York, Macmillan, 1949.

5.132   Murphy, Gardner, Historical Introduction of Modern Psychology, Revised Ed. New York, Harcourt Brace, 1949.

5.133   - - - Personality: A Biosocial Approach to Origins and Structure. New York, Harper, 1947.

5.134   - - - and Rensis Likert, Public Opinion and the Individual. New York, Harper, 1938.

5.135   Murphy, Gardner, Lois B. Murphy and Theodore M. Newcomb, Experimental Social Psychology. New York, Harper, 1937.

5.136   - - - , ed., Human Nature and Enduring Peace. Boston, Houghton Mifflin, 1945.

5.137   Murray, H. A., Thematic Apperception Test Manual, Cambridge, Harvard University Press, 1943.

5.138   Nadel, S. F., The Foundations of Social Anthropology. Glencoe, Ill., Free Press, 1951.

5.139   Newcomb, Theodore M. and E. L. Hartley, eds., Readings in Social Psychology. New York, Holt, 1937.

5.140   Nunez, Lucio Mendieta, Las Clases Sociales. Mexico, 1944.

5.141   Obrebski, J., "The Sociology of Rising Nations," International Social Science Bulletin, No. 2, 1952, pp. 238.

5.142   Odum, Howard, Understanding Society: The Principles of Dynamic Sociology. New York, Macmillan, 1947.

5.143   Park, Robert Ezra, Race and Culture. Glencoe, Ill., Free Press, 1950.

5.144   Parsons, Talcott, The Structure of Social Action. New York, McGraw-Hill, 1937.

5.145   - - - , Robert F. Bales and Edward A. Shils, Working Papers in the Theory of Action. Glencoe, Ill., Free Press, 1953.

5.146   - - - and Edward A. Shils, eds., Toward a General Theory of Action. Cambridge, Harvard University Press, 1951.

5.147   - - - "The Prospects of Sociological Theory," American Sociological Review, Vol. 15, 1950, pp. 3-16.

5.148   - - - "Racial and Religious Differences as Factors in Group Tensions," in L. Bryson et al., Eds., Approaches to National Unity, New York, Harper, 1945.

5.149   - - - and Bernard Barber, "Sociology, 1941-1946," in American Journal of Sociology, Vol. 53, No. 4, Jan. 1948, pp. 245-257.

5.150   Preuss, Konrad Theodor, Lehrbuch der Voelkerkunde. Stuttgart, Ferdinand Enke Verlag, 1937.

5.151   Recasens-Siches, Luis, Lecciones de Sociología. Mexico, Editorial Porrua, 1948.

5.152   Reik, T., Dogma and Compulsion. New York, International Universities Press, 1951.

5.153   Reuter, E. B., Race and Culture Contact. New York, McGraw-Hill, 1934.

5.154   Riegel, O. W., "Nationalism in Press, Radio and Cinema," American Sociological Review, Vol. 3, Aug. 1938, pp. 510-515.

5.155   Riesman, David, Faces in the Crowd. New Haven, Yale University Press, 1952.

5.155a   - - - Individualism Reconsidered. Glencoe, Ill., Free Press, 1954.

5.156   - - - and N. Glazer, The Lonely Crowd. New Haven, Yale University Press,1950.

5.157   - - - "Authority and Liberty in the Structure of Freud's Thought," Psychiatry: Journal for the Study of Interpersonal Processes, Vol. 13, No. 2, May 1950, pp. 167-188.

5.158   - - - "Some Observations Concerning Marginality," Phylon, Second Quarter, 1951.

5.159   - - - "Some Problems of a Course in Culture and Personality," Journal of General Education, Vol. 5, No. 2, Jan. 1951, pp. 122-136.

5.160   - - - "The Themes of Heroism and Weakness in the Structure of Freud's Thought," Psychiatry: Journal for the Study of Interpersonal Processes, Vol. 13, No. 3, Aug. 1950, pp. 301-316.

5.161   - - - "The Themes of Work and Play in the Structure of Freud's Thought," Psychiatry, Journal for the Study of Interpersonal Processes, Vol. 13, No. 1, Feb. 1950, pp. 1-16.

5.162   - - - and N. Glazer, "Social Structure, Character Structure, and Opinion," International Journal of Opinion and Attitude Research, Vol. 2, 1948, pp. 512-527.

5.163   Rose, Arnold M., ed., Race Prejudice and Discrimination. New York, Knopf, 1951.

5.164   Ruesch, J. and G. Bateson, Communication: The Social Matrix of Psychiatry. New York, McGraw-Hill, 1951.

5.165   - - - - - - "Structure and Process in Social Relations," Psychiatry, Vol. 12, No. 2, May 1949, pp. 105-124.

5.166   Salomon, G., ed., Nation und Nationalitaet, supplement to Jahrbuch fuer Soziologie. Karlsruhe, G. Braun, 1937. P.

5.167   Sapir, Edward, Selected Writings in Language, Culture, and Personality, ed. by D. G. Mandelbaum. Berkeley, University of California Press, 1949.

5.168   Schumpeter, Joseph A., Aufsätze zur Soziologie. Tübingen, J.C.B. Mohr (Paul Siebeck), 1953.

5.168a   - - - Imperialism and Social Classes, trans. Heinz Norden, ed. Paul M. Sweezy. New York, Kelley, 1951.

5.169   Shils, Edward A., The Present State of American Sociology. Glencoe, Ill., Free Press, 1948.

5.170   Skinner, B. F., Science and Human Behavior. New York, Macmillan, 1953.

5.171   Sorokin, Pitirim A., Social Mobility. New York, Harper, 1927.

5.172   - - - Society, Culture, and Personality: Their Structure and and Dynamics. New York, Harper, 1947.

5.173   - - - "War and Post-War Changes in Social Stratifications of the Euro-American Population," American Sociological Review, Vol. 10, No. 2, April 1945, pp. 294-303.

5.174   Stagner, R., "Correlational Analysis of Nationalistic Opinion," Journal of Social Psychology, Vol. 12, Aug. 1940, pp. 197-212.

5.175   - - - and C. E. Osgood, "Experimental Analysis of a Nationalistic Frame of Reference," Journal of Social Psychology, Vol. 14, Nov. 1941, pp. 389-401.

5.176   Stevens, S. S., ed., Handbook of Experimental Psychology. New York, Wiley, 1951.

5.177   Stoltenberg, Hans Lorenz, "Kurzer Abriss einer Geschichte der dutschen Soziologie," Weltwirtschaftliches Archiv, Jena, Vol. 31, 1930, pp. 53-72.

5.178   Stonequist, Everett V., The Marginal Man: A Study in Personality and Culture Conflict. New York, Scribners, 1937.

5.179   Strong, Edward W., "A Question of Interpretation," American Anthropologist, Vol. 50, 1948, pp. 216-224. A criticism of A. L. Kroeber's Configurations of Culture Growth.

5.180   Sturzo, Luigi, Inner Laws of Society. New York, Kennedy, 1944.

5.181   Taba, Hilda and William Van Til, Democratic Human Relations. Washington, D. C., National Council for Social Studies, Yearbook, 1946.

5.182   Thomas, W. I. and F. Znaniecki, The Polish Peasant in Europe and America, 2nd Ed., 2 vols. New York, University of Chicago Press, 1927.

5.183   Thompson, Laura, Culture in Crisis: A Study of the Hopi Indians. New York, Harper, 1950.

5.184   - - - "Logico-Aesthetic Integration in Hopi Culture," American Anthropologist, Vol. 47, No. 4, 1945, pp. 601-614.

5.185   - - - and Alice Joseph, The Hopi Way. Chicago, University of Chicago Press, 1945.

5.186   Thurnwald, Richard, Der Mensch geringer Naturbeherrschung. Berlin, De Gruyter, 1950.

5.187   - - - Partei und Klasse in Lebensprozess der Gessellschaft (Forschungen zur Volkerpsychologie and Soziologie, Vol. 2), Leipzig, 1926.

5.188   Thurston, L. L. and E. J. Chave, The Measurement of Attitudes. Chicago, University of Chicago Press, 1929.

5.189   - - - "An Experimental Study of Nationality Preferences," Journal of General Psychology, Vol. 1, 1928, pp. 405-425.

5.190   Tisdale, Hope, "The Process of Urbanization," Social Forces, Vol. 20, No. 3, March 1942, pp. 311-316.

5.191   Verhandlungen des Zweiten deutschen Soziologentages. Tuebingen, J.C.B. Mohr, 1913; discussions of nationalism. P.

5.192   Vidich, Arthur J., Political Factionalism in Palau: Its Rise and Development. Cambridge, June 1949. Multigraphed. Especially Chapter 5: "Social Change and Contemporary Factions," pp. 114-124.

5.193   Ware, Caroline, "Ethnic Communities," Encyclopedia of the Social Sciences, Vol. 5, New York, 1937, p. 607.

5.194   Weakland, John H., "Method in Cultural Anthropology," Philosophy of Science, Vol. 18, No. 1, Jan. 1951, pp. 55-69.

5.195   Weber, Max, Essays in Sociology, trans. by H. H. Gerth and C. W. Mills. New York, Oxford University Press, 1946.

5.196   - - - Gesammelte Aufsaetze zur Religionssoziologie, 3 vols., Tubingen, Mohr, 1923.

5.197   - - - Theory of Social and Economic Organization, trans. by A. M. Henderson and Talcott Parsons, New York, Oxford University Press, 1947.

5.198   Westermann, Diedrich, ed., Die heutigen Naturvoelker im Ausgleich mit der neuen Zeit. Stuttgart, Ferdinand Enke Verlag, 1940.

5.199   Wilson, George and Monica, Social Change. Cambridge, University Press, 1945.

5.200   Wirth, Louis, "Types of Nationalism," American Journal of Sociology, Vol. 41, May 1936, pp. 723-737.

5.201   Young, Kimball, Social Psychology. New York, Crofts, 1945.

5.202   Zawadski, B., "Limitations of the Scapegoat Theory of Prejudice," Journal of Abnormal and Social Psychology, Vol. 43, No. 2, 1948, pp. 127-141.

5.203   Znaniecki, Florian, "European and American Sociology after Two World Wars," American Journal of Sociology, Vol. 41, No. 3, November 1950, pp. 217-222.

6.   LINGUISTICS AND SOCIOLOGY AND POLITICS OF LANGUAGES
       AND SCRIPTS

6.1   Adelung, J. Charles and J. S. Vater, Mithridates. Berlin, Vossische
       Buchhandlung, 1809.

6.2   Aucamp, Anna Jacoba, Bilingual Education and Nationalism with
       Special Reference to South Africa. Pretoria, J. L. Van Schaik,
       1926. P.

6.3   Bloomfield, Leonard, Language. New York, Holt, 1933.

6.4   Bodmer, Frederick, The Loom of Language. New York, Norton,
       1944.

6.5   Bruggen, Carry van, Hedendaagsch Fetischisme. Amsterdam,
       E. Querido, 1948.

6.6   Diringer, David, The Alphabet: A Key to the History of Mankind.
       New York, Philosophical Library, 1948.

6.7   Drexel, A. and P. Wimpissinger, Atlas Linguisticus. Innsbruck,
       1934.

6.8   Finck, Franz Nikolaus, Die Sprachstaemme der Erde. Leipzig,
       Teubner, 1909.

6.9   Firth, John Rupert, The Tongues of Men. London, Watts, 1937.

6.10   Gamillschegg, Ernst, Die Sprachgeographie und Ihre Ergebnisse
       fuer die allgemeine Sprachwissenschaft. Leipzig, Velhagen &
       Klasing, 1928.

6.11   Goldstein, Kurt, Language and Language Disturbances: Aphasic
       Sympton Complexes and Their Significance for Medicine and
       Theory of Language. New York, Grune and Stratton, 1948.

6.12   Graff, W. L., Language and Languages. New York, Appleton,
       1932.

6.13   Groeber, Gustav, Grundriss der Romanischen Philologie.
       Strassburg, Truebner, 1906.

6.14   Grove, Victor, The Language Bar. London, Routledge & Paul,
       1950.

6.15   Haugen, Einar I., "The Origin and Early History of the New
       Norse Movement in Norway," Publications of the Modern
       Language Association, Vol. 48, No. 2, 1938, pp. 558-597.

6.16   Haugen, William Keith, Empire in the Changing World. New
       York, Penguin Books, 1943.

6.17   Havránek, Bohuslav, "Zum Problem der Norm in der heutigen
       Sprachwissenschaft und Sprachkultur," Actes du quatrième
       Congrès International de Linguistes (1936), Copenhagen, E. Munks-
       gaard, 1936, pp. 151-156.

6.18   Jakobson, Roman, Notes on General Linguistics: Its Present

40

State and Crucial Problems. July 1949. Unpublished.

6.19 - - - "The Beginnings of National Self-Determination in Europe," The Review of Politics, Vol. 7, No. 1, Jan. 1945, pp. 29-42.

6.20 - - - "Franz Boas' Approach to Language," International Journal of American Linguistics, Vol. 10, No. 4, Oct. 1944, pp. 188-195.

6.21 - - - "The Phonemic and Grammatical Aspect of Language in their Interrelations," Actes du 6e Congrès International de Linguistes, Paris, 1948.

6.22 - - - "Řeč a písemnictví Českých židů v době Přemyslovské," ms., unpublished.

6.23 - - - "Sur la theorie des affinités phonologiques des langues," Actes du quatrième Congrès International de Linguistes (1936), Copenhagen, E. Munksgaard, 1938, pp. 48-58.

6.24 - - - "Úvahy o básnictví doby Husitské," Slovo a slovesnost, Vol. 2, No. 1, 1936, pp. 1-21.

6.25 Jespersen, Otto, Language: Its Nature, Development and Origin. New York, Macmillan, 1949.

6.26 - - - Mankind, Nation and Individual from a Linguistic Point of View. Cambridge, Harvard University Press, 1925.

6.27 Kieckers, E., Die Sprachstaemme der Erde. Heidelberg, Winter, 1931.

6.28 Kloss, Heinz, "Sprachtabellen," Vierteljhresschrift fuer Politik und Geschichte, Vol. 1, No. 7, 1929, pp. 108-112.

6.28a Kučera, Jindřich, "Soviet Nationality Policy: The Linguistic Controversy," Problems of Communism, Vol. 3, No. 2 March-April 1954, pp. 24-29.

6.29 Laubach, Frank C., Teaching the World to Read: A Handbook for Literacy Campaigns. New York, Friendship Press, 1947.

6.30 Lenneberg, Erich H., "Cognition in Ethnolinguistics," Language, Vol. 29, No. 4, Oct.-Dec. 1953, pp. 463-471.

6.31 Meillet, A. and Marcel Cohen, Les Langues du Monde. Paris, Champion, 1924.

6.32 Neurath, Otto, International Picture Language. London, K. Paul Trench, Trubner, 1936.

6.33 Ogden, C. K., Debabelization. London, K. Paul, Trench, Trubner, 1931.

6.34 Ostwald, Wilhelm, Sprache und Verkehr. Leipzig, Akademische Verlagsgesellschaft, 1911.

6.35 Parker, William R., The National Interest and Foreign Languages: A Topic Selected for Examination in Citizen Consultations. Washington, U.S. Commission for UNESCO, 1954. With statistics.

6.36   Paul, Hermann, Principles of the History of Language. New York, Macmillan, 1889.

6.37   Pei, Mario A., The Story of Language. Philadelphia and New York, Lippincott, 1949.

6.38   - - - The World's Chief Languages, 3rd Ed. London, Allen & Unwin, 1949.

6.39   Pentillä, Aarni E., "Einige Bemerkungen ueber die Unterscheidung von Sprache und Rede," Actes du quatrième Congrès International de Linguistes, (1936).

6.40   Schlauch, Margaret, The Gift of Tongues. New York, Modern Age, 1942.

6.41   - - - "The Social Basis of Linguistics," Science and Society, Vol. 1, No. 1, Fall 1936, pp. 18-44.

6.42   Schmidt, Peter W., Die Sprachfamilien und Sprachenkreise der Erde. Heidelberg, Winter's Universitaets-buchhandlung, 1926.

6.43   Shenton, H. N., E. Sapir and O. Jespersen, International Communication. London, K. Paul, 1931.

6.44   Stalin, Joseph V., "On Marxism in Linguistics," Pravda, June 20, 1950; trans. in The Current Digest of the Soviet Press, Vol. II, No. 21, July 8, 1950, pp. 3-9.

6.45   - - - Marxism and Problems of Linguistics. New York, Four Continent Book Corporation, 1954.

6.46   Thorndike, E. L., "The Origin of Language," Science, Vol. 98, No. 2531, July 2, 1943, pp. 1-6.

6.47   UNESCO, Basic Facts and Figures: Illiteracy, Education, Libraries, Books, Newspapers, Newsprint, Film and Radio. Paris, UNESCO, 1952. (58 pp., and charts).

6.48   - - - Education in a Technological Society: A Preliminary International Survey of the Nature and Efficacy of Technical Education. Paris, UNESCO, 1952.

6.49   - - - Fundamental Education: A Description and Programs. Paris, UNESCO, 1949.

6.50   - - - Fundamental Education: A Quarterly Bulletin.

6.51   - - - The Teaching of Modern Languages: A Volume of Studies Deriving from the International Seminar Organized by the Secretariat of Unesco at Nuwara Eliya, Ceylon, in August 1953. Paris, Unesco, 1955.

6.52   - - - Trade Barriers to Knowledge: A Manual of Regulations Affecting Educational, Scientific and Cultural Materials. Paris, Unesco, 1951.

6.53   - - - Use of Vernacular in Education. Paris, Unesco, 1953.

6.54   - - - Women and Education. Paris, Unesco, 1953.

6.55   - - - World Communications: Press, Radio, Film. Report pro-
        duced under the direction of Albert A. Shea. New and rev. ed.
        Paris, Unesco, 1951.

6.56   - - - World Handbook of Educational Organization and Statistics.
        First Edition, 1951. Paris, Unesco, 1952.

6.57   - - - Progress of Literacy in Various Countries: A Preliminary
        Statistical Study of Available Census Data since 1900. New York,
        Columbia U. P., 1953, 224 p.

6.58   - - - World Survey of Education: Handbook of Educational Organi-
        zation and Statistics. New York, Columbia U.P., 1955, 900 p.

6.59   Vendryes, Joseph, Language: A Linguistic Introduction to History.
        New York, Knopf, 1925.

6.60   Vočádlo, Otakar, "Some Observations on Mixed Languages," Actes
        du quatrième Congrès International de Linguistes (1936), Copenhagen,
        E. Munksgaard, 1938, pp. 169-176.

6.61   Vossler, Karl, The Spirit of Language in Civilization. London,
        K. Paul, Trench, Trubner, 1932. P.

6.62   Wartburg, Walther von, Einfuehrung in die Problematik und
        Methodik der Sprachwissenschaft. Halle (Seale), Max Niemeyer
        Verlag, 1934.

6.63   Weinreich, Uriel, Languages in Contact: Findings and Problems.
        Publication of the Linguistic Circle of New York, No. 1, 1953,
        pp. xii-148. Summarizes and evaluates more than 600 publications
        pertaining to bilingualism, and offers formulations by the author.

6.64   Weisgerber, Leo, "Sprache und Begriffsbildung," Actes du quatrième
        Congrès International de Linguistes (1936), Copenhagen, E. Munks-
        gaard, 1938.

6.65   Wiener, Norbert, "The Mechanism of Language," and "The
        History of Language;" Chaps. 4 and 5 in The Human Use of Human
        Beings: Cybernetics and Society, Boston, Houghton Mifflin, 1950,
        pp. 85-103.

6.66   Wilson, Richard A., The Miraculous Birth of Language. London,
        Dent, 1945.

6.67   Woolner, A. C., Languages in History and Politics. London,
        Oxford University Press, 1938.

7.   HISTORY, GENERAL

7.1   Current History; special issue on Federalism, Vol. 16, No. 91, March 1949, pp. 131-166.

7.2   Bentley, Eric Russell, A Century of Hero Worship. Philadelphia, Lippincott, 1944.

7.3   Brinckley, Robert C., Realism and Nationalism, 1852-1871. New York and London, Harper, 1934.

7.4   Brinton, Crane, Ideas and Men: The Story of Western Thought. New York, Prentice-Hall, 1950.

7.5   Carr, E. H., The Soviet Impact on the Western World. New York, Macmillan, 1947.

7.6   - - - The Twenty Years Crisis, 1919-1939. London, Macmillan, 1939.

7.7   DeWitt, N. W., "Nationalistic Histories and World History," Royal Society of Canada Proceedings and Transactions, Series 3, Vol. 30, Section 2, 1936, pp. 1-6.

7.8   Enriques, F., "Importanza della Storia del Pensiero Scientifico nella Cultura Nazionale," Scientia, Vol. 63, March 1938, pp. 125-134. French tr. H. Buriot-Darsiles Vol. 63, Sup. March 1938, pp. 47-56.

7.9   Fay, Sidney B., Origins of the World War. New York, Macmillan, 1934, 2 vols.

7.10   Hadas, M., "Aspects of Nationalist Survival under Hellenistic and Roman Imperialism," Journal of the History of Ideas, Vol. 11, April 1950, pp. 131-139.

7.11   Koht, Halvdan, "The Dawn of Nationalism in Europe," American Historical Review, Vol. 52, No. 2, Jan. 1947, pp. 265-280.

7.12   Hayes, Carlton, A Generation of Materialism, 1871-1900. New York, Harper, 1941.

7.13   - - - The Historical Evolution of Modern Nationalism. New York, Macmillan, 1948.

7.14   Hölzle, E., "Das Zeitalter der Völker," Historische Zeitschrift, Vol. 160, No. 3, 1939, pp. 480-495.

7.15   Kantorowicz, Ernst, "Pro Patria Mori in Medieval Political Thought," The American Historical Review, Vol. 56:3, April 1951, pp. 472-492.

7.16   Kirn, Paul, Aus der Frühzeit des Nationalgefühls.

7.17   - - - Politische Geschichte der deutschen Grenzen, Leipzig, Bibliog. Institut, 1943.

7.18   Kohn, Hans, Prophets and Peoples: Studies in Nineteenth Century Nationalism. New York, Macmillan, 1945. Contains an outstanding study of Treitschke.

7.19   - - - Revolutions and Dictatorships: Essays in Contemporary History. Cambridge, Harvard University Press, 1941.

7.20   - - - "End of 1848," Current History, Vol. 16 (New Series), May 1949, pp. 276-280: Twentieth Century, Vol. 146, Sept. 1949, pp. 174-185.

7.21   - - - "Napoleon and the Age of Nationalism," Journal of Modern History, Vol. 22, No. 1, March 1950, pp. 21-37.

7.22   - - - "The Roots of Modern Nationalism," in Bulletin of the International Committee of the Historical Sciences, Paris, Presses Universitaires, 1938, pp. 388-391.

7.23   Langer, William L., The Diplomacy of Imperialism, 1890-1902. New York, Knopf, 1951, 2 vols.

7.24   - - - European Alliances and Alignments, 1871-1890. New York, Knopf, 1950.

7.25   Lemberg, Eugen, Geschichte des Nationalismus in Europe. Stuttgart, Schwabe, 1951. A short survey stressing the importance of historical and political events in welding a nation.

7.26   Mitscherlich, Waldemar, Nationalismus: Die Geschichte einer Idee. Leipzig, Hirschfeld, 1929. P.

7.27   Rosenstock, Huessy Eugen, Out of Revolution: Autobiography of Western Man. New York, Morrow, 1938.

7.28   Rothfels, H., "1848: One Hundred Years After," Journal of Modern History, Vol. 20, Dec. 1948, pp. 291-319.

7.29   Schuman, F. L., Europe on the Eve: The Crises of Diplomacy, 1933-1939. New York, Knopf, 1939.

7.30   - - - Night Over Europe: The Diplomacy of Nemesis, 1939-1940. New York, Knopf, 1941.

7.31   Toynbee, Arnold J., A Study of History. London, Oxford University Press, 1931-1954, 10 vols.

7.32   Vossler, Otto, Der Nationalgedanke von Rousseau bis Ranke. München und Berlin, Verlag von R. Oldenbourg, 1937.

7.33   Walsh, Gerald Groveland, S.J., Dante Alighieri, Citizen of Christendom. Milwaukee, Bruce Publishing, 1946.

7.34   Wartburg, Walther von, Les Origines des Peuples Romans. Paris, Presses Universitaires, 1941.

7.35   Zatschek, Heinz, Das Volksbewusstsein: sein Werden im Spiegel der Geschichtsschreibung. Brunn, Vienna Leipzig, 1936.

7.36   Zöllner, Erich, Die Politische Stellung der Völker im Frankenreich. Vienna, Universum Verlagsgesselschaft, 1950.

8. ECONOMIC HISTORY Including Urbanization, History of Population Changes and Income Changes

8.1 Angell, Norman, The Great Illusion. New York, Putnam, 1913.

8.2 - - - Raw Materials, Population Pressure and War. Boston, World Peace Foundation, 1936.

8.3 Ashton, Thomas S., The Industrial Revolution. London, Oxford University Press, 1948.

8.4 Bonn, Moritz J., The Crumbling of Empire: The Disintegration of World Economy. London, Allen & Unwin, 1938.

8.5 Brady, Robert A., Business as a System of Power. New York, Columbia University Press, 1943.

8.6 Brentano, Lujo, Die Anfaenge des modernen Kapitalismus, Munich, Akademie der Wissenschaften, 1916.

8.7 Buck, Philip W., The Politics of Mercantilism. New York, Holt, 1942.

8.8 Carr-Saunders, A. M., and P. A. Wilson, The Professions. Oxford Carendon Press, 1933.

8.9 Childe, V. G., What Happened in History. New York, Penguin Books, 1946.

8.10 Clark, Grover, The Balance Sheets of Imperialism: Facts and Figures on Colonies. New York, Columbia University Press, New York, Columbia University Press, 1936.

8.11 Deutsch, Karl W., "Medieval Unity and the Economic Conditions for an International Civilization," Canadian Journal of Economics and Political Science, Feb. 1944, pp. 18-35.

8.12 Eldridge, Seba, et al., Development of Collective Enterprise: Dynamics of an Emergent Economy. Lawrence, Kan., University Press, 1943.

8.13 Giedion, Siegfried, Mechanization Takes Command: A Contribution to Anonymous History. New York, Oxford University Press, 1948.

8.14 - - - Space, Time, and Architecture. Cambridge, Harvard University Press, 1948.

8.15 Heckscher, Eli F., The Continental System: An Economic Interpretation. Oxford, Clarendon Press, 1922.

8.16 - - - Mercantilism. London, Allen & Unwin, 1935, 2 vols.

8.17 - - - "A Plea for Theory in Economic History," Economic History, Vol. 1, Jan. 1929, pp. 524-534.

8.18 Innis, Harold A., The Bias of Communication. Toronto, University of Toronto Press, 1951.

8.19 - - - Empire and Communication. Oxford, Clarendon Press, 1950.

8.20　　- - -, ed., Essays in Transportation in Honor of W. T. Jackson.
Toronto, University Press, 1941.

8.21　　Innis, Mary Q., An Economic History of Canada. Toronto, Ryerson
Press, 1935.

8.22　　Jenks, Leland H., Migration of British Capital to 1875. New York,
Knopf, 1938.

8.23　　Mumford, Lewis, The Culture of Cities. New York, Harcourt,
Brace, 1938.

8.24　　- - - Technics and Civilization. New York, Harcourt, Brace,
1934, 1947.

8.25　　Polanyi, Karl, The Great Transformation. New York, Farrar and
Rinehart, 1944.

8.26　　Power, Eileen, Medieval People, 9th Ed. New York, Barnes and
Noble, 1950.

8.27　　Schulte, Aloys, Geschichte des mittelalterlichen Handels und
Verkehrs zwischen Westdeutschland und Italien. Leipzig, Duncker
& Humblot, 1900, 2 vols.

8.28　　Scoville, Warren C., "Minority Migrations and the Diffusion of
Technology," Bureau of Business and Economic Research, Los
Angeles, University of California, 1951, pp. 347-361.

8.29　　Sombart, Werner, Der Bourgeois: Zur Geistesgeschichte des
modernen Wirtschaftsmenschen. Munich-Leipzig, Duncker &
Humblot, 1920.

8.30　　- - - Der moderne Kapitalismus: historischsystematische
Darstellung des gesamteuropaeischen Wirtschaftslebens von
seinen Anfaengen bis zur Gegenwart. Munich-Leipzig, Duncker
& Humblot, 1928, 1927, 3 vols. in 6.

8.31　　- - - "Capitalism," Encyclopedia of the Social Sciences, Vol. 3,
New York, Macmillan, 1930, pp. 195-208.

8.32　　Staley, Eugene, War and the Private Investor: A Study in the
Relations of International Politics and Internations Private
Investment. Garden City, Doubleday, Doran, 1935.

8.33　　United Nations Statistical Office, Data on Urban and Rural Popu-
lations in Recent Censuses. New York, 1950, U.N. Publications
Sales No. 1950. XIII. 4.

8.34　　- - - National and Per Capita Incomes of Seventy Countries in
1949. U.N. St/Stat/Ser.E/1, New York, Oct. 1950. More recent
data were published in the United Nations Monthly Bulletin of
Statistics, Vol. 6, No. 6, June 1950.

8.35　　Usher, Abbott Payson, "The Application of Quantitative Methods
to Economic History," Journal of Political Economy, Vol. 40,
No. 2, April 1932, pp. 186-209.

8.36   - - - "Population and Settlement in Eurasia," Geographical Review, New York, Vol. 20, 1930, pp. 110-132.

8.37   - - - "Soil Fertility, Soil Exhaustion, and their Historical Significance," Quarterly Journal of Economics, Vol. 37, May 1923, pp. 385-411.

8.38   Viner, Jacob, "Power Versus Plenty as Objectives of Foreign Policy in the Seventeenth and Eighteenth Centuries," World Politics, Vol. 1, No. 1, Oct. 1948.

8.39   Weber, Max, General Economic History. New York, Greenberg, 1927. Glencoe, Ill., Free Press, 1950.

8.40   Wittfogl, K. A., Die Geschichte der Buergerlichen Gesellschaft. Vienna-Berlin, Malik, 1924.

9.   ECONOMICS AND ECONOMIC POLICY Including Population Theory,
        Income Theory and Economic Development

9.1   Abraham, W. I., "The Distribution of World Income," The Ameri-
        can Statistician, April-May 1951, p. 39.

9.2   American Economic Association, Readings in the Theory of
        International Trade, Selected by a Committee of the American
        Economic Association. Philadelphia, Blakiston, 1949.

9.3   Auld, G. P., "Economic Nationalism vs. World Recovery," Vital
        Speeches, Vol. 3, Feb. 15, 1937, pp. 267-270.

9.4   Balogh, Thomas, The Dollar Crisis, Causes and Cure: A Report
        to the Fabian Society, Oxford, Blackwell, 1950.

9.5   Bente, Hermann, "Die marktwirtschaftliche Bedeutung der Kapital-
        anlage im Auslande," Weltwirtschaftliches Archiv, Jena, Vol. 32,
        1930, II, pp. 1-54.

9.6   Beveridge, Sir William, Tariffs: The Case Examined. London,
        Longmans Green, 1931.

9.7   Bloomfield, A. I., Speculative and Flight Movements of Capital
        and Postwar International Finance. Princeton, Princeton Univer-
        sity Press, 1954.

9.8   Boulding, Kenneth E., Economic Analysis. New York, Harper,
        1941.

9.9   - - - The Economics of Peace. New York, Prentice-Hall, 1945.

9.10   - - - A Reconstruction of Economics. New York, Wiley, 1950.

9.11   Boyd-Orr, John and David Lubback, The White Man's Dilemma:
        Food and the Future. London, Allen & Unwin, 1953.

9.12   Brocard, Lucien, "Die lokale und regionale Wirtschaft als Grund-
        lage der Volks und Weltwirtschaft," Weltwirtschaftliches Archiv,
        Jena, Vol. 31, 1930, pp. 35-52.

9.13   Brown, Harrison, The Challenge of Man's Future. New York,
        Viking, 1954.

9.14   Carver, T. N., "Economic Basis of Nationalism; With Discussion,"
        Institute of World Affairs, Proceedings, Vol. 17, 1939, pp. 27-30,
        55-57.

9.15   Chamberlin, E. H., "Monopolistic Competition Revisited," Econ-
        omica, Vol. 18 (New Series), No. 72, Nov. 1951, pp. 343-362.

9.16   - - - The Theory of Monopolistic Competition, 3rd Ed. Cambridge,
        Harvard University Press, 1935.

9.17   Clark, Colin, The Conditions of Economic Progress. London,
        Macmillan, 1949.

9.18   - - - The Economics of 1960. London, Macmillan, 1942.

9.19   - - - "Economic Life in the Twentieth Century," Measure, Vol. 1,

No. 4, Fall 1950, pp. 329-347.

9.20   Colm, Gerhard, "Das Gesetz der Komparativen Kosten -- das
        Gesetz der komparativen Kaufkraft," Weltwirtschaftliches Archiv,
        Jena, Vol. 3, 1930, II, pp. 371-405.

9.21   Commons, John R., Institutional Economics. New York, Macmillan,
        1934.

9.22   Condliffe, J. B., The Commerce of Nations. New York, Norton,
        1950.

9.23   Creamer, Daniel, ed., Bibliography on Income and Wealth, Vol I,
        1937-1947. Cambridge, Bowes and Bowes, 1952.

9.24   Deane, Phyllis, ed., Bibliography on Income and Wealth, Vol. II,
        1948-1949. Cambridge, Bowes and Bowes, 1953.

9.25   - - - Bibliography on Income and Wealth, Vol. III, 1950. Cam-
        bridge, Bowes and Bowes, 1953.

9.26   Delaisi, Francis, Political Myths and Economic Realities. London,
        Noel Douglas, 1927. P.

9.27   Deutsch, Karl W., "The Economic Factor in Intolerance," in
        L. Bryson et al., eds., Approaches to National Unity, New York,
        Harper, 1945, pp. 368-386.

9.28   - - - "Some Economic Aspects of the Rise of Nationalistic and
        Racial Pressure Groups," Canadian Journal of Economics and
        Political Science, Vol. 8, No. 1, Feb. 1942, pp. 109-115.

9.29   Dobb, Maurice, Political Economy and Capitalism. London,
        Routledge, 1935.

9.30   "Economic Growth: A Symposium," Journal of Economic History,
        Supplement 7, 1947.

9.31   "Economics and War," Round Table, Vol. 25, June 1935, pp.
        524-534.

9.32   Engliš, Karel, Regulierte Wirtschaft. Prague, Orbis Verlag,
        1936.

9.33   Feiler A., "Economic Nationalism," Annals of the American
        Academy of Political and Social Science, Vol. 180, July 1935,
        pp. 203-206.

9.34   Gini, Corrado, Trans. by Robert K. Merton, "Problems of the
        International Distribution of Population and Raw Materials,"
        Annals of the American Academy of Political and Social Science,
        Vol. 189, Jan. 1937, pp. 201-214.

9.35   Haberler, G. F., The Theory of International Trade, with Its
        Application to Commercial Policy. New York, Macmillan, 1937.

9.36   Hamilton, Walton, The Pattern of Competition. New York,
        Columbia University Press, 1940.

9.37   Hansen, Alvin H., and Harvey S. Perloff, Regional Resource
        Development. Washington, National Planning Association, 1942.

9.38   Harris, Seymour E., Economic Planning: The Plans of Fourteen
        Countries with Analyses of the Plans. New York, Knopf, 1949.

9.39   - - - Exchange Depreciation: Its Theory and Its History, 1931-
        1935, with some Consideration of Related Domestic Policies.
        Cambridge, Harvard University, 1936.

9.40   - - - The New Economics: Keynes' Influence on Theory and
        Public Policy. New York, Knopf, 1947.

9.41   Hatt, Paul K., ed., World Population and Future Resources:
        Proceedings of the Second Centennial Academic Conference of
        Northwestern University. New York, American Book Co., 1952.

9.42   Hawtrey, E. G., Economic Aspects of Sovereignty. London,
        Longmans Green, 1930.

9.43   Hayek, Friedrich A. von, Monetary Nationalism and International
        Stability. London, Longmans, Green, 1937.

9.44   - - - "Kapitalaufzehrung," Weltwirtschaftliches Archiv, Jena,
        Vol. 36, 1932, II, pp. 86-108.

9.45   Heimann, Eduard, History of Economic Doctrines: An Introduction
        to Economic Theory. New York, Oxford University Press, 1945.

9.46   Heuser, Heinrich, Control of International Trade. Philadelphia,
        Blakiston, 1939.

9.47   Higgins, Benjamin, What do Economists Know: Six Lectures on
        Economics in the Crisis of Democracy. Melbourne, Melbourne
        University Press, 1951.

9.48   Hilferding, Rudolf, Das Finanzkapital. Vienna, Wiener Volksbuch-
        handlung, 1923.

9.49   Hoselitz, R. F., ed., The Progress of the Underdeveloped Areas.
        Chicago, University of Chicago Press, 1952.

9.50   Hurwicz, Leonid, and Jacob Marschak, Games and Economic
        Behavior: Two Review Articles. Cowles Commission Papers,
        (New Series) No. 13, Cowles Commission for Research in Econ-
        omics. Chicago, University of Chicago Press, 1946.

9.51   International Labor Office, Indigenous Peoples: Living and Work-
        ing Conditions of Aboriginal Populations in Independent Countires.
        Geneva, International Labor Office, 1953.

9.52   Isaac, Julius, Economics of Migration. London, K. Paul, Trench,
        Trubner, 1947.

9.52 a Isard, Walter and Guy Freutel, "Regional and National Product
        Projections and their Interrelations," in National Bureau of
        Economic Research, Conference on Research in Income and
        Wealth, Long-Range Economic Projection: Studies in Income and

Wealth, Vol. 16, Princeton, Princeton University Press, 1954, pp. 427-471.

9.53 - - -,"The General Theory of Location and Space-Economy," Quarterly Journal of Economics, Vol. 63, Nov. 1949, pp. 476-506.

9.54 - - - "Some Empirical Results and Problems of Regional Input-Output Analysis," in Wassily W. Leontief, Studies in the Structure of the American Economy: Theoretical and Empirical Explorations in Input-Output Analysis, New York, Oxford University Press, 1953.

9.54a - - - and Guy Fruetal, "Regional and National Product Projections and Their Interrelations," in Long-Range Economic Projection: Studies in Income and Wealth. A report of the National Bureau of Economic Research, Princeton, Princeton University Press, 1954, pp. 427-471.

9.55 Keynes, John Maynard, The Economic Consequences of the Peace. New York, Harcourt, Brace and Howe, 1920.

9.56 - - - The End of Laissez-Faire. London, Hogarth, 1926.

9.57 - - - Essays in Persuasion. New York, Harcourt, Brace, 1932.

9.58 - - - The General Theory of Employment, Interest, and Money. New York, Harcourt, Brace, 1936.

9.59 Kindleberger, Charles Poor, The Dollar Shortage. Cambridge, Massachusetts Institute of Technology Press, 1950.

9.60 - - - "Group Behavior and International Trade," Journal of Political Economy, Vol. 59, No. 1, Feb. 1951, pp. 30-46.

9.61 Kuznets, Simon Smith, National Income: A Summary of Findings. New York, National Bureau of Economic Research, Inc., 1946.

9.62 - - - "Measurement," in "Economic Growth: A Symposium," Journal of Economic History, Supplement 7, 1947, pp. 10-34.

9.63 - - - "The State as a Unity in the Study of Economic Growth," Journal of Economic History, Vol. 11, No. 1, Winter 1951, pp. 25-41.

9.64 Lamb, Robert K., "Productivity and Social Structure," Industrial Productivity, Industrial Relations Research Association, pp. 50-75.

9.65 League of Nations, Commercial Policy in the Inter-War Period. Geneva, 1942.

9.66 - - - Quantitative Trade Controls, Their Causes and Nature. Geneva, 1942.

9.67 Lenin, V. I., Imperialism, The Highest Stage of Capitalism. "New Data," edited by E. Varga and E. Mendelsohn. New York, International Publishers, n.d., 1936-1937.

9.68 Leontief, Wassily, et al., Studies in the Structure of the American Economy: Theoretical and Empirical Explorations in Input-Output Analysis. New York, Oxford University Press, 1953; especially "interregional theory," pp. 93-115.

9.69   Lösch, A., Die räumliche Ordnung der Wirtschaft. Jena, 1944.

9.70   Maclaurin, W. R., "The Process of Technological Innovation," American Economic Review, Vol. 40, No. 1, March 1950, pp. 90-113.

9.71   Machlup, Fritz, International Trade and the National Income Multiplier. Philadelphia, Blakiston, 1943.

9.72   - - - "Die Theorie der Kapitalflucht," Weltwirtschaftliches Archiv, Jena, Vol. 36, 1932, II, pp. 512-529.

9.73   Manoilescu, Mihail, The Theory of Protection and International Trade. London, King, 1931.

9.74   Marshall, Alfred, Official Papers. London, Macmillan, 1926.

9.75   Marx, Karl, Capital: A Critique of Political Economy. New York, Modern Library, 1936.

9.76   - - - and Friedrich Engels, Historische Kritische Gesamtausgabe: Werke, Schriften, Briefe, D. Rjazanov, ed. Berlin, Marx Engels Verlag, 1927-1935.

9.77   Muehlenfels, Albert von, "Der Kolonialbegriff in der Wirtschafts-wissenschaft," Weltwirtschaftliches Archiv, Jena, Vol. 56, 1942, II, pp. 28-60.

9.78   Nadler, M., "Economic Interdependence: Present and Future," American Economic Review, Vol. 27, Supplement, March 1937, pp. 1-11.

9.79   National Bureau of Economic Research, Problems in the Study of Economic Growth, New York, National Bureau of Economic Research, Inc., 1949. Multigraphed.

9.80   Notestein, F. W., et al., The Future Population of Europe and the Soviet Union: Population Projections 1940-1970. (Geneva, League of Nations, 1944; publ. No. 1944, II A. 2.) "Selected Bibliography on Population Projections," pp. 219-234.

9.81   Nurkse, Ragnar, Problems of Capital Formation in Underdeveloped Countries. New York, Oxford University Press, 1953.

9.82   Ohlin, Bertil, "Protection and Non-competing Groups," Welt-wirtschaftliches Archiv, Jena, Vol. 33, 1931, I, pp. 30-45.

9.83   - - - International and Interregional Trade. Cambridge, Harvard University Press, 1933.

9.83a   Organization for European Economic Co-operation, Com-ments on the Strasbourg Plan, Chateau de la Muette, May 1954.

9.84   Pigou, A. C., Economics in Practice: Six Lectures on Current Issues. London, Macmillan, 1935.

9.85   - - - The Economics of Welfare, 3rd Ed. London, Macmillan, 1929.

9.86   - - - Essays in Applied Economics. London, King, 1923.

9.87   - - - The Political Economy of War, New & Rev. Ed. London, Macmillan, 1940.

9.88   - - - Protection and Preferential Import Duties, New York, Macmillan, 1906.

9.89   - - - Socialism vs. Capitalism. London, Macmillan, 1937.

9.89a   Polak, Jacques J., "Conceptual Problems Involved in Projections of the International Sector of Gross National Product," in National Bureau of Economic Research, Conference on Research in Income and Wealth, Long-Range Economic Projection: Studies in Income and Wealth, Vol. 16, Princeton, Princeton University Press, 1954, pp. 377-423.

9.90   Reder, A. M., "Inter-Temporal Relations of Demand and Supply within the Firm," Canadian Journal of Economics and Political Science, Vol. 7, Feb. 1941, pp. 26-30.

9.91   Robbins, Lionel, Economic Aspects of Federation. London, Macmillan, 1941.

9.92   - - - The Economic Causes of War. London, Cape, 1939.

9.93   - - - Economic Planning and International Order. London, Macmillan, 1937.

9.94   - - - The Economic Problem in Peace and War. London, Macmillan, 1947.

9.95   Robinson, Joan, The Economics of Imperfect Competition. London, Macmillan, 1933.

9.96   Roepke, Wilhelm, "Die saekulare Bedeutung der Weltkrisis," Welwirtschaftliches Archiv, Jena, Vol. 37, 1931, pp. 1-27.

9.97   Roll, Erich, A History of Economic Thought, Rev. Ed. New York, Prentice-Hall, 1942.

9.98   Rostow, Walt Whitman, The Process of Economic Growth. New York, Norton, 1952.

9.99   - - - "Government and Private Enterprise in European Recovery," Journal of Economic History, Supplement X, 1950, pp. 105-113.

9.100   - - - "The Historical Analysis of the Terms of Trade," Economic History Review, 2nd Ser., Vol. 4, No. 1, 1951, pp. 53-76.

9.101   - - - "Some Notes on Mr. Hicks and History," American Economic Review, Vol. 41, No. 3, June 1951, pp. 316-334.

9.102   - - - "The Terms of Trade in Theory and Practice," Economic History Review, 2nd Ser., Vol. 3, No. 1, 1950, pp. 1-20.

9.103   - - - "The United Nations' Report on Full Employment," The Economic Journal, London, Vol. 60, No. 238, June 1950, pp. 323-350.

9.104   Salin, Edgar, "Von den Wandlungen der Weltwirtschaft in der Nachkriegszeit," Weltwirtschaftliches Archiv, Jena, Vol. 34, 1932, pp. 1-33.

9.105   Salz, Arthur, "Die Zukunft des Imperialismus," Weltwirtschaftliches Archiv, Jena, Vol. 3, 1930, II, pp. 317-348.

9.106   Samuelson, Paul Anthony, Economics: An Introductory Analysis. New York, McGraw-Hill, 1948.

9.107   - - - Foundations of Economic Analysis, New York, McGraw-Hill, 1948.

9.108   - - - "International Trade and the Equalization of Factor Prices," The Economic Journal, London, Vol. 48, 1948, pp. 163 ff.; and "International Factor Price Equalization once Again," Ibid., Vol. 59, 1949, p. 181 ff.

9.109   - - - "Welfare, Economics and International Trade," American Economics Review, Vol. 23, No. 2, June 1938, pp. 261-266.

9.110   - - - and Wolfgang F. Stolper, "Protection and Real Wages," Review of Economic Studies, Vol. 9, No. 1, Nov. 1941.

9.111   Sayre, F. B., "Menace of Economic Nationalism," Academy of Political Science Proceedings, Vol. 16, Jan. 1935, pp. 206-214.

9.112   - - - "Problem of Underdeveloped Areas in Asia and Africa," American Academy of Arts and Sciences Proceedings, Vol. 81, No. 6, 1952, pp. 284-298.

9.113   Schumpeter, Joseph A., Capitalism, Socialism and Democracy. New York, Harper, 1942.

9.114   - - - History of Economic Analysis. New York, Oxford University Press, 1954.

9.115   - - - Imperialism and Social Classes. New York, Kelley, 1951.

9.116   - - - The Theory of Economic Development. Cambridge, Harvard University Press, 1936.

9.117   Sievers, A. M., Has Market Capitalism Collapsed? A Critique of Karl Polanyi's New Economics. New York, Columbia University Press, 1949.

9.118   Smith, J. G., "Economic Nationalism and International Trade," Economic Journal, Vol. 45, Dec. 1935, pp. 619-648.

9.119   Soule, George, Introduction to Economic Science. New York, Viking, 1948.

9.120   Staley, Eugene, The Future of Underdeveloped Countries. New York, Harper, 1954.

9.121   Sulzbach, Walter, Nationales Gemeinschaftsgefuehl and Wirtschaftliches Interesse. Leipzig, Hirschfeld, 1929. P.

9.122   - - - "Der wirtschaftliche Begriff des 'Auslands'," Weltwirtschaftliches Archiv, Jena, Vol. 32, 1930, II, pp. 55-80.

9.123   Sweezy, Paul M., The Theory of Capitalist Development: Prin-
        ciples of Marxism Political Economy. New York, Oxford Univer-
        sity Press, 1942.

9.124   Taft, Philip, Movements for Economic Reform. New York,
        Reinhart, 1950.

9.125   Taussig, F. M., International Trade. New York, Macmillan, 1927.

9.126   Veblen, Thorstein, Absentee Ownership and Business Enterprise
        in Recent Times: The Case of America. New York, Viking, 1945.

9.127   - - - The Place of Science in Modern Civilization, and Other
        Essays. New York, Huebsch, 1919.

9.128   - - - The Theory of Business Enterprise. New York, Scribner,
        1920.

9.129   Victor, Max, "Das sogenannte Gesetz der abnehmenden Aussen-
        handelsbedeutung," Weltwirtschaftliches Archiv, Jena, Vol. 36,
        1932, II, pp. 59-85.

9.130   Viner, Jacob, The Customs Union Issue. New York, Carnegie
        Endowment for International Peace, 1950; "Bibliography,"
        pp. 171-211.

9.130a - - - International Economics. Glencoe, Free Press, 1951.

9.131   - - - Studies in the Theory of International Trade. New York,
        Harper, 1937.

9.132   Von Neumann, John, and Oskar Morgenstern, Theory of Games
        and Economic Behavior. Princeton, Princeton University Press,
        1947.

9.133   Weber, Alfred, The Theory of the Location of Industries. Chicago,
        University of Chicago Press, 1929.

9.134   Weber, Max, Der Nationalstaat und die Volkswirtschaftspolitik.
        Leipzig, Mohr, 1895.

9.135   Weigmann, Hans, "Ideen zu einer Theorie der Raumwirtschaft.
        Ein Versuch zur Begruendung einer realistischen Wirtschafts-
        theoric," Weltwirtschaftliches Archiv, Jena, Vol. 34, 1931, III,
        pp. 1-40.

9.135a Williamson, Harold F. and John A. Buttrick, eds., Economic
        Development Principles and Patterns. New York, Prentice-
        Hall, 1954.

9.136   Zimmerman, Erich, World Resources and Industries: Appraisal
        of the Availability of Agricultural and Industrial Materials, Rev.
        Ed. New York, Harper, 1951.

9.137   - - - "The Resource Hierarchy of Modern World Economy,"
        Weltwirtschaftliches Archiv, Jena, Vol. 33, 1931, I, pp. 431-463.

10.   GEOGRAPHY, GEOPOLITICS AND REGIONAL PLANNING

10.1   Boggs, S. Whittemore, International Boundaries. New York, Columbia University Press, 1940. A study of boundary functions and problems.

10.2   - - - "Geographic and Other Scientific Techniques for Political Science," American Political Science Review, Vol. 42, No. 2, April 1948, pp. 223-238; especially interesting list of proposed studies on pp. 235-237.

10.3   Bowman, Isaiah, The New World: Problems in Political Geography, 4th Ed. New York, World Book Co., 1928.

10.4   Brunhes, Jean and Camille Veilleux, La Geographie de l'histoire. Paris, Alcan, 1921. P.

10.5   Cornish, Vaughn, Borderlands of Language in Europe and their Relation totthe Historic Frontier of Christendom. London, Sifton, Praed, 1936.

10.6   - - - The Great Capitals: An Historical Geography. London, Methuen, 1923.

10.7   de Castro, Josue, The Geography of Hunger. Boston, Little, Brown, 1952.

10.8   Dickinson, Robert E., City Region and Regionalism: A Geographical Contribution to Human Ecology. New York, Oxford University Press, 1947.

10.9   Dorpalen, Andreas, The World of General Haushofer: Geopolitics in Action. New York, Farrar & Rhinehart, 1942.

10.10   Fairgrieve, James, Geography and World Power, Rev. Ed. New York, Dutton, 1935.

10.11   Gyorgy, Andrew, Geopolitics: The New German Science. Berkeley, University of California Press, Berkeley, 1944.

10.12   - - - "The Application of German Geopolitics: Geo-Sciences," American Political Science Review, Vol. 37, No. 4, Aug. 1943, pp. 677-685.

10.13   Hartshorne, Richard, The Nature of Geography. Ann Arbor, Edwards, 1946.

10.14   - - - "Recent Developments in Political Geography," American Political Science Review, Vol. 29, Nos. 5 and 6, Oct. and Dec. 1935, pp. 785-804, 943-966.

10.15   Haushofer, Albrecht, Zur Problematic des Raumbegriffes. Berlin, Grunewald, Vowinckel, 1932.

10.16   Haushofer, Karl, Geopolitik der Pan-Ideen. Berlin, Zentral Verlag, 1931. P.

10.17   - - - Grenzen in ihrer geographischen und politischen Bedeutung, Rev. Ed. Heidelberg, Vowinckel, 1939.

10.18   - - - Weltpolitik von Heute, Rev. Ed. Berlin, Andermann, 1937.

10.19   - - - , et al., Zur Geopolitik der Selbstbestimmung: Suedostas-
iens Wiederaufstieg zur Selbstbestimmung. Munich, Roesl &
Cie, 1923.

10.20   - - - , ed., Weltwirtschaftsdaemmerung, Festschrift zum zehnjaehri-
gen Bestehen des Weltwirtschaftsinstitutes der Handelshochschule
Leipzig. Stuttgart, Kohlhammer, 1934.

10.21   Huntington, Ellsworth, Mainsprings of Civilization. New York,
Wiley, 1945.

10.22   - - - and S. W. Cushing, Principles of Human Geography, 6th Ed.,
a revision by Earl B. Shaw. New York, Wiley, 1951.

10.23   James, Preston E., A Geography of Man. Boston, Ginn, 1939;
with bibliographical "References," pp. 574-580.

10.24   Jones Stephen Barr, Boundary-Making: A Handbook for States-
men, Treaty Editors and Boundary Commissioners, with a foreword by S. Whittemore Boggs. Washington, Carnegie Endowment
for International Peace, 1945.

10.25   MacKinder, Sir Halford J., Democratic Ideals and Reality: A
Study in the Politics of Reconstruction. New York, Holt, 1942.

10.26   - - - "The Geographical Pivot of History," Geographical Journal,
Vol. 23, 1904, pp. 421-444.

10.27   Mattern, Johannes, Geopolitik: Doctrine of National Self-Suf-
Sufficiency and Empire. Baltimore Johns Hopkins University
Press, 1942.

10.28   Mess, H. A., "Geography in Relation to National and Local Sentiment," Sociological Review, Vol. 30, April 1938, pp. 186-200.

10.29   Moore, H. E., "Regionalism and Permanent Peace," Social
Forces, Vol. 23, Oct. 1944, pp. 15-19.

10.30   Neumann, Siegmund, "Fashions in Space," Foreign Affairs,
Vol. 21, No. 2, Jan. 1943, pp. 276-288.

10.31   Peattie, Roderick, Look to the Frontiers: A Geography for the
Peace Table.

10.32   Ratzel, Friedrich, Politische Geographie, 2nd Ed. München,
Oldenbourg, 1903.

10.33   Sargent, Arthur John, Seaports and Hinterlands. London, Black,
1938.

10.34   Shaw, C. F., "Is Nationalism Promoting Erosion?" Geographical
Review, Vol. 26, Jan. 1936, pp. 149-150.

10.35   Shepherd, William R., Historical Atlas, 7th Ed. New York, Holt,
1929.

10.36   Spykman, Nicholas John, The Geography of the Peace. New York,
Harcourt-Brace, 1944.

10.37   Taylor, Griffith, Environment and Nation. Chicago, University
        of Chicago Press, 1936.

10.38   - - -, ed., Geography in the Twentieth Century. New York,
        Philosophical Library, 1951.

10.39   Van Cleef, E., "Cities and Nationalism," Scientific Monthly,
        Vol. 47, Oct. 1938, pp. 341-343.

10.40   Van Valkenburg, Sammuel, Elements of Political Geography.
        New York, Prentice-Hall, 1939.

10.41   - - - Peace Atlas of Europe. New York, Duell, Sloan and Pearce,
        1946.

10.42   Weigert, Hans Werner, Generals and Geographers: The Twilight
        of Geopolitics. New York, Oxford University Press, 1942.

10.43   - - - German Geopolitics. New York, Oxford University Press,
        1942.

10.44   - - - and V. Stefansson, eds., New Compass of the World: A
        Symposium on Political Geography. New York, Macmillan, 1944.

10.45   Whittlesey, Derwent, The Earth and the State: A Study of Political
        Geography. New York, Holt, 1939.

10.46   - - - Environmental Foundations of European History. New York,
        Appleton-Century-Crofts, 1949.

11.   BIOLOGY: GENTICS: RACE.

11.1   Ashley-Montagu, M. F., Darwin: Competition and Cooperation. New York, Schuman, 1952.

11.2   - - - An Introduction to Physical Anthropology, 2nd Ed. Springfield, Thomas, 1951.

11.3   - - - Man's Most Dangerous Myth: The Fallacy of Race, 2nd Ed. New York, Columbia University Press, 1945.

11.4   - - - On Being Human. New York, Schuman, 1950.

11.5   - - - Statement on Race. New York, Schuman, 1951. "A Select Annotated List of Books and Pamphlets on Race," pp. 159-165.

11.6   - - - "Racism, the Bomb and the World's People," Asia, Vol. 46, Dec. 1946, pp. 535-545.

11.7   Barnett, Anthony, The Human Species. New York, Norton, 1950.

11.8   Barzun, Jacques, Race: A Study in Modern Superstition. New York, Harcourt-Brace, 1937.

11.9   Benedict, Ruth, Race: Science and Politics. New York, Modern Age Books, 1940.

11.10   - - - and G. Weltfish, The Races of Mankind. New York, Public Affairs Committee, Inc., 1943.

11.11   Boas, Franz, The Mind of Primitive Man, rev. ed. New York, Macmillan, 1938.

11.12   - - - Race and Democratic Society. New York, Augustin, 1945.

11.13   - - - Race, Language and Culture. New York, Macmillan, 1940.

11.14   Boyd, William Clouser, Genetics and the Races of Man: An Introduction to Modern Physical Anthropology. Boston, Little, Brown, 1950.

11.15   Brown, J. C., Race Relations in a Democracy. New York, Harper, 1949.

11.16   Coon, Carleton Stevens, Stanley M. Garn, and Joseph B. Birdsell, Races. Springfield, Ill., Thomas, 1950.

11.17   Dahlberg, Gunnar, Race, Reason, and Rubbish: A Primer of Race Biology. New York, Columbia University Press, 1942.

11.18   Dover, Cedric, Know This of Race. London, Secker and Warburg, 1939.

11.19   Dunn, L. C., and T. Dobzhansky, Heredity, Race, and Society. New York, Penguin Books, 1946.

11.20   Haldane, J. B. S., Heredity and Politics. New York, Norton, 1938.

11.21   Hogben, Lancelot, "Race and Prejudice," in Dangerous Thoughts, New York, Norton, 1940.

11.22   Hooton, Ernest Albert, Twilight of Man. New York, Putnam, 1939.

60

11.23   Huxley, Julian H., Evolution in Action. New York, Harper, 1953.

11.24   - - - Evolution: The Modern Synthesis. New York, Harper, 1943.

11.25   - - - Man in the Modern World. New York, New American Library, 1948.

11.26   - - - Man Stands Alone. New York, Harper, 1941.

11.27   - - - "Race" in Europe. New York, Farrar, 1939.

11.28   - - - and A. C. Haddon. We Europeans: A Survey of "Racial" Problems. New York, Harper, 1936.

11.29   Klineberg, Otto, Race Differences. New York, Harper, 1935.

11.30   - - - "Racial Psychology," in R. Linton, Ed., The Science of Man in the World Crisis. New York, Columbia University Press, 1945, pp. 63-77.

11.31   Krogman, W. M., "The Concept of Race," in R. Linton, Ed., The Science of Man in the World Crisis. New York, Columbia University Press, 1945, pp. 38-62.

11.32   Myers, Henry A., Are Men Equal? New York, Putnam, 1945.

11.33   Rashevsky, Nicolas, Mathematical Biology of Social Behavior. Chicago, University of Chicago Press, 1951.

11.34   - - - Mathematical Theory of Human Relations: An Approach to a Mathematical Biology of Social Phenomena. Bloomington, Ind.

11.35   Scheinfeld, Amram, The New You and Heredity. Philadelphia, Lippincott, 1950.

11.36   Snyder, Louis L., Race: A History of Modern Ethnic Theories. New York, Toronto, Longmans Green, 1939.

11.37   Voegelin, Eric, "The Growth of the Race Idea," Review of Politics, Vol. 2, No. 3, July 1940, pp. 283-317.

12.   RELIGION AND RELIGIOUS ORGANIZATIONS

12.1   Anon, "Beyond Nationalism," Commonweal, Vol. 47, March 5, 1948, pp. 508-509. "Exaggerated nationalism, has a flushed, unhealthy, and specious aspect now, which may well signify very near dissolution. The war and post-war years furnish much more evidence proclaiming deep weakening of nationalism than a truly climactic strength."

12.2   - - - "Holy Father Condemns Exaggerated Nationalism," Catholic World, Vol. 147, Sept. 1938, pp. 747-748.

12.3   - - - "Nationalism and Missions," Christian Century, Vol. 57, March 20, 1940, p. 375.

12.4   - - - "Post Nationalism," Commonweal, Vol. 48, June 4, 1948, p. 176. "For Christians, certainly, the ideal is the 'Planetary Christianity' which increasingly seems the only alternative to no-Christianity."

12.5   Baron, Salo W., Modern Nationalism and Religion. New York, Harper, 1947. A broad inquiry into the general problem, by an outstanding authority on Jewish social history. Interesting data on different religions and nationalistic movements are also given in the notes.

12.6   Brown, S. J., "Concerning Nationality," Catholic World, Vol. 152, Feb. 1941, pp. 542-546.

12.7   - - - "Nationalism True and False," Catholic World, Vol. 150, Jan. 1940, pp. 432-438.

12.8   - - - "Principle of Nationalities," Catholic World, Vol. 155, July 1942, pp. 416-421.

12.9   Buber, M., "Beginning of the National Idea; Rabbi Loew ben Bezalel's Specifically Jewish Philosophy of History," Review of Religion, Vol. 10, March 1946, pp. 254-265.

12.10   de la Bedoyere, M., "Heresy of Nationalism," Catholic World, Vol. 151, July 1940, pp. 487-489.

12.11   Ellul, J., "On the Cultural and Social Factors Influencing Church Division (Conservatism and the Political Situation)," Ecumenical Review, Vol. 4, April 1952, pp. 269-275.

12.12   Furfey, P. H., "Curse of Nationalism," Catholic World, Vol. 156, March 1943, pp. 652-657.

12.13   Gallagher, Buell, G., Color and Conscience. New York, Harper, 1946.

12.14   Gillis, J. M., "This Aryan Madness," Catholic World, Vol. 47, Sept. 1938, pp. 641-647.

12.15   Hayes, Carlton H., "The Church and Nationalism - A Plea for Further Study of a Major Issue," The Catholic Historical Review, Vol. 28, No. 1, April 1942, Washington, D. C., pp. 1-12.

12.16   - - - "Revival of Tribalism," Christian Century, Vol. 53, Jan. 22, 1936, p. 174.

12.17   Krauder, E., "Holy Ghost and the National Spirit; Study in Secularization," Virginia Quarterly Review, Vol. 26, No. 1, Jan. 1950, pp. 44-60.

12.18   Murray, J., "Nationalism: Genuine, Extreme," Catholic World, Vol. 145, April 1937, pp. 104-105.

12.19   Norem, R. A., "Is the National State Obsolete?" Christian Century, Vol. 54, Oct. 6, 1937, pp. 1226-1228.

12.20   North, E. M., The Book of a Thousand Toungues. New York, Harper, 1938.

12.21   Northcott, C., "Passing of Foreign Missions (Caused by the Pressures of Modern Nationalism," Religion in Life, Vol. 22, No. 4, 1953, pp. 587-593.

12.22   Oldham, Joseph H., Christianity and the Race Problem. London, Christianity and the Race Problem, 1925.

12.23   Pius XII, "Charitable Peace; Idolatry of Nationalism Condemned," Vital Speeches, Vol. 11, April 1, 1945, pp. 357-359.

12.24   Poling, Paul Newton, ed., God and the Nations. Garden City, Doubleday, 1950.

12.25   Rau, Enrique, El racismo national socialista y el Christianismo. Buenos Aires, Gladium, 1939.

12.26   Scotford, J. R., "Nations are Like Denominations," Christian Century, Vol. 53, July 1, 1936, pp. 932-933.

12.27   Wilkins, E. H., "Ties that Bind," Christian Century, Vol. 62, Nov. 21, 1945, pp. 1282-1284.

12.28   Wittram, Reinhard, Nationalismus und Säkularisation. Lüneberg, Heliand-Verlag, 1949.

12.29   Workman, H. B., "Political Issues of the Reformation," London Quarterly Review, Vol. 161, Oct. 1936, pp. 433-438.

13   PHILOSOPHIC AND ETHICAL ASPECTS

13.1   Burnes, C. D., "Making the International Mind," Ethics, Vol. 36, pp. 137-146.

13.2   Kaye, M., "Exclusive State and Goodness," Sociological Review, Vol. 32, Jan. 1940, pp. 64-84.

13.3   Kohn, Hans, "Ahad Ha'am: Nationalist with a Difference," Commentary, June 1951, pp. 558-566.

13.4   - - - "Zionism," in Hans Kohn's Revolution and Dictatorships, Harvard University Press, 3rd Printing, 1943, pp. 399-430.

13.5   Kulischer, Eugen, Jewish Migrations: Past Experiences and Post-War Prospects. New York, The American Jewish Committee, 1943.

13.6   Morris, C. W., The Open Self. New York, Prentice-Hall, 1949.

13.7   - - - "The Comparative Strength of Life Ideals in Eastern and Western Culture," in Charles A. Moore Ed., Essays in East-West Philosophy, Honolulu, University of Hawaii Press, 1951.

13.8   Negley, G., "Values, Sovereignty, and World Law," Ethics, Vol. 60, April 1950, pp. 208-214.

13.9   Tauber, Kurt P., "Nationalism and Self-Defense," Ethics, Vol. 62, July 1952, pp. 275-281.

13.10   Viereck, Peter, "The Revolution in Values: Roots of the European Catastrophe, 1870-1952," Political Science Quarterly, Vol. 67, 1952, pp. 338-356.

14	SPECIFIC PEOPLES, AREAS AND PROBLEMS
14.1	UNITED STATES
14.1.1	Some General Bibliographies and Surveys.
14.1.1.1	Adamic, Louis, A Nation of Nations. New York, Harper, 1944.
14.1.1.2	Brown, Francis J., and Joseph S. Roucek, eds., One America. New York, Prentice-Hall, 1945.
14.1.2	General Works on Nationalism.
14.1.2.1	Almond, Gabriel H., The American People and Foreign Policy. New York, Harcourt, Brace, 1950. Discusses U. S. Foreign Policy since the 1930's in connection with the "American National Character", using many quantitative results of public opinion polls.
14.1.2.2	Beard, Charles A., The Idea of National Interest: An Analytical Study of American Foreign Policy. New York, Macmillan, 1934. P.
14.1.2.3	- - - The Open Door at Home: A Trial Philosophy of National Interest. New York, Columbia University Press, 1934.
14.1.3	Political Science.
14.1.3.1	Anon., "Future of U. S. Foreign Policy; We Must Adopt a Revolutionary Principle to Escape the Conflict between Industrialism and Nationalism," Fortune, Vol. 23, May 1941, pp. 54-55.
14.1.3.2	Catlin, G. E. G., Anglo-Saxony and Its Tradition. New York, Macmillan, 1939.
14.1.3.3	- - - One Anglo-American Nation: . . . Anglo-Saxony as Basis of World Federation: A British Response to Streit. London, Dakers, 1941.
14.1.3.4	Cohn, D. L., "Isolation: The Dodo," Atlantic Monthly, Vol. 164, Aug. 1939, pp. 155-162.
14.1.3.5	Cook, T. I., and M. Moos, "The American Idea of International Interest," American Political Science Review, Vol. 47, No. 1, March 1953, pp. 28-44.
14.1.3.6	Holcombe, Arthur N., The Middle Class in American Politics. Cambridge, Harvard University Press, 1940. Considers the widespread identification of the American people with its middle classes as a source of political stability. For possible middle class propensities to instability or violence, see e. g. F. Neumann; T.F. Abel; C. Wright Mills; and D. Riesman.
14.1.3.7	- - - Our More Perfect Union. Cambridge, Harvard University Press, 1950.
14.1.3.8	Kirk, G., "Declining Empires and American Interests,"

Survey and Survey Midmonthly, Vol. 85, May 1949, pp. 254-258.

14.1.3.9   Myrdal, Gunnar, An American Dilemma: The Negro Problem and Modern Democracy. New York, Harper, 1919.

14.1.3.10   Ranney, John C., "The Bases of American Federalism," The William and Mary Quarterly, Vol. 3, No. 1, Jan. 1946, pp. 1-35.

14.1.3.11   Record, Wilson, The Negro and the Communist Party. Chapel Hill, University of North Carolina Press, 1951.

14.1.3.11a - - - "The Negro Intellectual and Negro Nationalism," Social Forces, Vol. 33, No. 1, Oct. 1954, pp. 10-18.

14.1.3.12   Ross, Malcolm, All Manner of Men. New York, Reynal and Hitchcock, 1948.

14.1.3.13   Spykman, Nicholas John, America's Strategy in World Politics: The United States and the Balance of Power. New York, Harcourt, Brace, 1942.

14.1.3.14   - - - The Balance of Tomorrow: Power and Foreign Policy in the United States. New York, Putnam, 1945.

14.1.3.15   Thompson, Carol, "A More Perfect Union," Current History, Vol. 16, No. 91, March 1949, pp. 136-142 (United States).

14.1.3.16   Van Alstyne, Richard W., American Crisis Diplomacy. Stanford, Stanford University Press, 1952.

14.1.3.17   Wilson, F. C., "The Revival of Organic Theory," American Political Science Review, Vol. 36, June 1942, pp. 454-459 (American Nationalism).

14.1.5   Cultural Anthropology, Sociology and Social Psychology.

14.1.5.1   Bruner, Jerome S., Mandate from the People. New York, Duell, Sloan and Pearce, 1944.

14.1.5.2   Child, Irvin L., Italian or American? The Second Generation in Conflict. New Haven, Yale University Press, 1943.

14.1.5.3   Christowe, Stoyan, This is My Country: An Autobiography. New York, Carrick and Evans, 1938.

14.1.5.4   Deutsch, Morton, and M. E. Collins, Interracial Housing: A Psychological Evaluation of a Social Experiment. Minneapolis, University of Minnesota Press, 1951.

14.1.5.5   Dollard, John, Caste and Class in a Southern Town. New Haven, Yale University Press, 1938.

14.1.5.6   Forster, Arnold, A Measure of Freedom: An Anti-Defamation League Report. New York, Doubleday, 1950.

14.1.5.7   Gorer, Geophrey, The American People: A Study in National Character. New York, Norton, 1948.

14.1.5.8   Guilford, J. P., "Racial Preferences of a Thousand Ameri-
            can University Students," Journal of Social Psychology,
            Vol. 2, 1931, pp. 179-204.

14.1.5.9   Hart, Hornell, Selective Migration as a Factor in Child
            Welfare in the United States with Special Reference to
            Iowa. Iowa City, University of Iowa, 1921.

14.1.5.10   Holingshead, August B., Elmtown's Youth: The Impact of
            Social Classes on Adolescents. New York, Wiley, 1949.

14.1.5.11   Kardiner, Abraham, and L. Ovesey, The Mark of Oppression:
            A Psycholosocial Study of the American Negro. New York,
            Norton, 1951.

14.1.5.12   Katz, Daniel, and Kenneth Braly, "Racial Stereotypes of
            One Hundred College Students," Journal of Abnormal and
            Social Psychology, Vol. 28, 1933, pp. 280-290.

14.1.5.13   Klineberg, Otto, ed., Characteristics of the American Negro.
            New York, Harper, 1944.

14.1.5.14   Kracauer, Siegfried, "National Types as Hollywood Presents
            Them," Public Opinion Quarterly, Vol. 13, 1949, pp. 53-72.

14.1.5.15   Kriesberg, Martin, "Soviet News in the 'New York Times',"
            Public Opinion Quarterly, Vol. 10, 1946, pp. 540-565.

14.1.5.16   Landis, K. M., Segregation in Washington: A Report of the
            National Committee on Segregation in the Nation's Capital.
            1948.

14.1.5.17   McDonagh, E. C. and Eugene S. Richards, Ethnic Relations
            in the United States. New York, Appleton-Century-Crofts, 1953.

14.1.5.18   Mead, Margaret, And Keep Your Powder Dry. New York, Mor-
            row, 1942.

14.1.5.19   Powdermaker, Hortense, "An Anthropologist Looks at the
            Movies," Annals of the American Academy of Political and
            Social Science, Vol. 254, 1947, pp. 80-87.

14.1.5.20   - - - "The Channeling of Negro Aggression by the Cultural
            Process," American Journal of Sociology, Vol. 58, 1943,
            pp. 750-758.

14.1.5.21   Ross, Arthur M., "The Negro Worker in the Depression,"
            Social Forces, Vol. 18, No. 4, May 1940, pp. 550-559.

14.1.5.22   Schermerhorn, R. A., These Our People. Boston, Heath,
            1949.

14.1.5.23   Severson, A. L., "Nationality and Religious Preferences as
            Reflected in Newspaper Advertisements," American Journal
            of Sociology, Vol. 44, 1939, pp. 540-545.

14.1.5.24   Thomas, Dorothy Swaine, et al., Japanese American Evac-
            uation and Resettlement: The Salvage. Berkeley, University
            of California Press, 1952.

14.1.5.25   - - - and Richard B. Nishimoto, Japanese American Evacuation and Resettlement: The Spoilage. Berkeley, University of California Press, 1946.

14.1.5.26   Warner, William Lloyd, et al., Social Class in America: A Manual of Procedure for the Measurement of Social Status. Chicago, Science Research Associates, 1949.

14.1.5.27   - - - and P. Lunt, The Social Life of a Modern Community. New Haven, Yale University Press, 1941.

14.1.5.28   - - - and - - - The Status System of a Modern Community. New Haven, Yale University Press, 1942.

14.1.5.29   - - - and Leo Srole, The Social Systems of American Ethnic Groups. New Haven, Yale University Press, 1946.

14.1.5.30   Wilson, H. E., Latin America in School and College Teaching Material. Washington, D. C., American Council on Education, 1944.

14.1.5.31   - - - Treatment of Asia in American Textbooks. New York, American Council of the Institute of Pacific Relations, 1946.

14.1.5.32   Wolfenstein, Martha, and Nathan Leites, "An Analysis of Themes and Plots," Annals of the American Academy of Political and Social Science, Vol. 254, 1947, pp. 41-48.

14.1.6   Linguistics; Sociology and Politics of Languages and Scripts.

14.1.6.1   Mencken, H. L., The American Language, 4th Ed. New York, Knopf, 1937.

14.1.7   History, General.

14.1.7.1   Beard, Charles A., The Rise of American Civilization. New York, Macmillan, 1937.

14.1.7.2   Bemis, Samuel Flagg, A Diplomatic History of the United States, 3rd Ed. New York, Holt, 1950.

14.1.7.3   Bridenbaugh, Carl, Seat of Empire: The Political Role of Eighteenth-Century Williamsburg. Williamsburg, Colonial Williamsburg, Inc., 1950.

14.1.7.4   Commager, Henry S., The American Mind. New Haven, Yale University Press, 1950.

14.1.7.5   Curti, Merle, The Roots of American Loyalty. New York, Columbia Press, 1946.

14.1.7.6   Daykin, W. L., "Nationalism as Expressed in Negro History," Social Forces, Vol. 13, Dec. 1934, pp. 257-263.

14.1.7.7   Dodd, William E., The Cotton Kingdom: A Chronicle of the Old South. New Haven, Yale University Press, 1919.

14.1.7.8   Frazier, Franklin E., The Negro in the United States. New York, Macmillan, 1949.

14.1.7.9   Hacker, Louis H., ed., The Shaping of the American Tradi-
              tion. New York, Columbia University Press, 1947.

14.1.7.10   Logan, Rayford W., The Negro in American Life and Thought:
              The Nadir, 1877-1901. New York, Dial Press, 1954.

14.1.7.11   Morison, S. E., and H. S. Commager, The Growth of the
              American Republic, 3rd Ed. New York, Oxford University
              Press, 1942. 2 vols.

14.1.7.12   Parrington, Vernon Louis, Main Currents in American
              Thought: An Interpretation of American Literature from
              the Beginnings to 1920. New York, Harcourt, Brace, 1930.
              3 vols. in 1.

14.1.7.12a   Potter, David M., People of Plenty: Economic Abundance
              and the American Character. Chicago, The University of
              Chicago Press, 1954.

14.1.7.13   Robson, C. B., "Francis Lieber's Nationalism," Journal
              of Politics, Vol. 8, Feb. 1946, pp. 47-73.

14.1.7.14   Saveth, E. N., "Race and Nationalism in American Historio-
              graphy: The Late Nineteenth Century," Political Science
              Quarterly, Vol. 54, Sept. 1939, pp. 421-441.

14.1.7.15   Tryon, W. S., "Nationalism and International Copyright,
              Tennyson and Longfellow in America," American Literature,
              Vol. 24, Nov. 1952, pp. 301-309.

14.1.7.16   Warfel, Harry R., Noah Webster, Schoolmaster to America
              New York, Macmillan, 1936.

14.1.7.17   Wecter, Dixon, The Hero in America. New York, Scribner,
              1941.

14.1.7.18   Weinberg, Albert, Manifest Destiny. Baltimore, Johns
              Hopkins Press, 1935.

14.1.8   Economic History.

14.1.8.1   Arnold, Thurman, The Bottlenecks of Business. New York,
              Reynal and Hitchcock, 1940.

14.1.8.2   Beard, Charles A., An Economic Interpretation of the Consti-
              tution of the United States. New York, Macmillan, 1913.

14.1.8.3   Burns, Arthur R., The Decline of Competition: A Study of
              the Evolution of American Industry. New York, McGraw-
              Hill, 1936.

14.1.8.4   Hacker, Louis, The Triumph of American Capitalism: The
              Development of Forces in American History to the End of
              the Nineteenth Century. New York, Simon and Schuster,
              1940.

14.1.8.5   Harris, Abram L., The Negro as Capitalist: A Study of
              Banking and Business among American Negroes.

Philadelphia, American Academy of Political and Social Science, 1936.

14.1.8.6   Mitchell, Broadus, and Louis Pearson Mitchell, American Economic History. Boston, Houghton Mifflin, 1947.

14.1.8.7   - - - Depression Decade: From New Era to New Deal. New York, Rinehart, 1947.

14.1.8.8   Ruehl, Alfred, Vom Wirtschaftsgeist in Amerika. Leipzig, Quelle & Meyer, 1927.

14.1.8.9   Taussig, F. M., Some Aspects of the Tariff Question: An Examination of the Development of American Industries under Protection, 3rd Ed. Cambridge, Harvard University Press, 1931.

14.1.8.10   Williamson, Harold F., ed., The Growth of the American Economy: An Introduction to the Economic History of the United States. New York, Prentice-Hall, 1947.

14.1.8.11   Wright, Chester W., Economic History of the United States. New York, McGraw-Hill, 1941.

14.1.9   Economics and Economic Policy.

14.1.9.1   Hansen, Alvin H., America's Role in the World Economy. New York, Norton, 1945.

14.1.9.2   Perloff, Harvey S., Puerto Rico's Economic Future: A Study in Planned Development. Chicago, University of Chicago Press, 1950.

14.1.10   Geography, Geopolitics and Regional Planning.

14.1.10.1   National Resources Committee, Our Cities: Their Role in the National Economy. Washington, D. C., U.S. Government Printing Office, June 1937.

14.1.10.2   Odum, Howard, Southern Regions of the United States. Chapel Hill, University of North Carolina Press, 1936.

14.1.10.3   - - - The Way of the South: Toward the Regional Balance of America. New York, Macmillan, 1947.

14.1.11   Biology; Genetics; Race.

14.1.11.1   Dreher, C., "Racism and America's World Position: The Potential of Democratic Nationalism," (Reply to F. Munz) Commentary, Vol. 4, Aug. 1947, pp. 164-169.

14.1.21   Miscellaneous

14.1.21.1   Copland, Aaron, Our New Music. New York, McGraw, 1941.

14.2   GREAT BRITAIN, THE COMMONWEALTH AND IRELAND

14.2.1   Some General Bibliographies and Surveys.

14.2.1.1   Comstock, Alzada, "Commonwealth and Empire," Current
            History, Vol. 16, No. 91, March 1949, pp. 162-166.

14.2.1.2   Griffith, Llewelyn Wyn, The Welsh. London, Penguin Books,
            1949.

14.2.1.3   - - - The Welsh and Their Country. London, Longmans.

14.2.1.4   Rhys, Sir John, et al., The Welsh People: Chapters on their
            Origin, . . . Language, Literature and Characteristics,
            4th Ed. London, Allen and Unwin, 1906.

14.2.2   General Works on Nationalism.

14.2.2.1   Attwater, D., "Welsh Nationalism," Commonweal, Vol. 29,
            Jan. 27, 1939, pp. 374-376.

14.2.2.2   Brady, Alexander, "The British Commonwealth: A Sympos-
            ium, Part 3, Nationalism and Democracy in the British
            Commonwealth: Some General Trends," American Political
            Science Review, Vol. 47, No. 4, Dec. 1953, pp. 1029-1040.

14.2.2.3   Duffus, Robert Luther, "Clues to an Understanding of John
            Bull," New York Times Magazine, Aug. 20, 1950, p. 41.

14.2.2.4   Humphreys, E. M., "Welsh Nationalism and Its Background,"
            Fortnightly, Vol. 150 (New Series Vol. 144), Aug. 1938,
            pp. 146-152.

14.2.2.5   MacKirdy, K. A., "Problems of Adjustment in Nation Build-
            ing," Canadian Journal of Economics and Political Science,
            Vol. 20, No. 1, Feb. 1954, pp. 27-43.

14.2.3   Political Science.

14.2.3.1   Brady, Alexander, Democracy in the Dominions: A Com-
            parative Study in Institutions. New York, Oxford University
            Press, 1952.

14.2.3.2   Fowler, R. M., Confederation Marches On: A Comment
            on the Rowell Sirois Report. Toronto, Canadian Institute
            of International Affairs, 1940.

14.2.3.3   Hancock, William Keith, Empire in the Changing World.
            New York, Penguin Books, 1944.

14.2.3.4   - - - Survey of British Commonwealth Affairs; Vol. 1,
            Problems of Nationality 1918-1936. London, Oxford
            University Press, 1937.

14.2.3.5   Mansergh, Nicholas, The Commonwealth and the Nations:
            Studies in British Commonwealth Relations. London,
            Royal Institute of International Affairs, 1948.

14.2.3.6   - - -, ed., Documents and Speeches on British Common-
            wealth Affairs, 1931-1952. New York, Oxford University

Press, 1953.

14.2.3.7   Martin, Kingsley, The Magic of Monarchy. New York, Knopf, 1937.

14.2.3.8   Russell, George William ("AE"), The Economics of Ireland and the Policy of the British Government. New York, Huebsch, 1920.

14.2.39   - - - The National Being: Some Thought on an Irish Polity. New York, Macmillan, 1916.

14.2.5   Cultural Anthropology, Sociology and Social Psychology.

14.2.5.1   Arensberg, Conrad M., and Solon T. Kimball, Family and Community in Ireland. Cambridge, Harvard University Press, 1940.

14.2.5.2   O' Faolain, Sean, The Irish: A Character Study. New York, Devin-Adair, 1949.

14.2.5.3   Silberman, L., and B. Spice, Colour and Class in Six Liverpool Schools. Liverpool, University Press of Liverpool, 1950.

14.2.6   Linguistics, Sociology and Politics of Language and Scripts.

14.2.6.1   Baker, Sidney John, Australia Speaks: A Supplement to "The Australian Language." Sydney, London, New York, Shakespeare Head Press, 1953.

14.2.6.2   - - - The Australian Language. Sydney, London, Angus and Robertson, 1945.

14.2.6.3   - - - Australian Pronunciation, A Guide to Good Speech. Sydney, Angus and Robertson, 1947.

14.2.6.4   Brogan, Mary Cogan, "Linguistic Nationalism in Eire," Review of Politics, Vol. 3, 1941, pp. 225-242.

14.2.6.5   Craigie, W. A., et al., The Scottish Tongue. London, Cassell, 1924.

14.2.6.6   Great Britain, Board of Education, Committee on Welsh in the Educational System of Wales, Welsh in Education and Life. London, 1927.

14.2.6.7   Richards, I. A., Basic English and Its Uses. New York, Norton, 1943.

14.2.6.8   Tagget, J. H., English in the Future. London, Nelson, 1940.

14.2.6.9   Wyld, H. C., A Short History of English, 3rd Ed. New York, Dutton, 1937.

14.2.7   History, General.

14.2.7.1   Beer, Max, History of British Socialism. London, Allen and Unwin, 1948. 1 vol. ed.

14.2.7.2   Bell, Herbert C., Lord Palmerston. London, Longmans

Green, 1936. 2 vols.

14.2.7.3   Brown, George W., "Canadian Nationalism: An Historical Approach," International Affairs, Vol. 30, No. 2, April 1954, pp. 166-174.

14.2.7.4   Burt, A. L., "The American Key," Revue de l'Université d'Ottawa, Vol. 12, No. 2, April-June 1942, pp. 3-16.

14.2.7.5   Cole, G. D. H., A Short History of the British Working-Class Movement, 1789-1947, New Ed. London, Allen and Unwin, 1948.

14.2.7.6   Gibb, Andrew Dewar, Scottish Empire. London, Maclebose, 1937.

14.2.7.7   Gleason, John Hawes, The Genesis of Russophobia in Great Britain. Cambridge, Harvard University Press, 1950.

14.2.7.8   Hyde, Douglas, A Literary History of Ireland. London, Unwin, 1903.

14.2.7.9   Knorr, Klaus E., British Colonial Theories, 1570-1850. Toronto, University of Toronto Press, 1944.

14.2.7.10   Kohn, Hans, "Genesis and the Character of English Nationalism," Journal of the History of Ideas, Vol. 1, No. 1, Jan. 1940, pp. 69-94.

14.2.7.11   MacDermot, Frank, Theobald Wolfe Tone. London, 1939.

14.2.7.12   Martin, Kingsley, The Triumph of Lord Palmerston. New York, MacVeagh, Dial Press, 1924.

14.2.7.13   Temperley, H. W. V., The Foreign Policy of Canning, 1822-1827: England, the Neo-Holy Alliance and the New World. London, Bell, 1925.

14.2.7.14   Wade-Evans, A. W., et al., The Historical Basis of Welsh Nationalism: A Series of Lectures. Cardiff, Plaid Cymru, 1950.

14.2.7.15   Ward, Sir Adolphus William and G. P. Gooch, eds., The Cambridge History of British Foreign Policy, 1783-1919. Cambridge, University Press, 1922-1923.

14.2.7.16   Webster, C. K., The Foreign Policy of Castlereagh, 1812-1815: Britain and the Reconstruction of Europe. London, Bell, 1931.

14.2.8.   Economic History.

14.2.8.1   Bonn, Moritz J., Die Englische Kolonisation in Irland. Stuttgart, Berlin, Cotta, 1906.

14.2.8.2   Brebner, J. Bartlet, "Laissez Faire and State Intervention in Nineteenth Century Britain," Journal of Economic History, Supplement VIII, 1948, pp. 59-73.

14.2.8.3   Chart, D. A., An Economic History of Ireland. Dublin, Talbot Press, 1920.

14.2.8.4   - - - The Story of Dublin. London, Dent, 1932.

14.2.8.5   Clapham, J. H., A Concise Economic History of Britain: From the Earliest Times to 1750. Cambridge, University Press, 1949.

14.2.8.6   - - - An Economic History of Modern Britain. Cambridge, University Press, 1926-1938. 3 vols.

14.2.8.7   Davies, D. J., The Economic History of South Wales Prior to 1850. Cardiff, 1933.

14.2.8.8   Dietz, F. C., An Economic History of England. New York, Holt, 1942.

14.2.8.9   Dobb, Maurice, Studies in the Development of Capitalism. London, Routledge, 1946.

14.2.8.10   Glazebrook, G. P. de T., "Nationalism and Internationalism on Canadian Waterways," in H. K. Innis, Ed., Essays in Transportation in Honour of W. T. Jackson, Toronto, University of Toronto Press, 1941.

14.2.8.11   Grant, Isabel Frances, The Economic History of Scotland. London, Longmans, Green, 1934.

14.2.8.12   Hammond, J. L., The Town Labourer, 1760-1932: The New Civilization. London, Longmans, Green, 1917.

14.2.8.13   - - - The Village Labourer, 1760-1832: A Study in the Government of England Before the Reform Bill. London, Longmans, Green, 1911.

14.2.8.14   - - - and Barbara Hammond, The Skilled Labourer, 1760-1832. London, Longmans, Green, 1919.

14.2.8.15   Hoffman, Ross, J. S., Great Britain and the German Trade Rivalry, 1875-1914. Philadelphia, 1933.

14.2.8.16   Jones, Evan J., Some Contributions to the Economic History of Wales. London, King, 1928.

14.2.8.17   MacDonald, D. F., Scotland's Shifting Population, 1770-1850. Glasgow, Jackson, 1937.

14.2.8.18   Redford, Arthur, The Economic History of England, 1760-1860. London, Longmans, Green, 1931.

14.2.8.19   Rostow, Walt Whitman, The British Economy of the Nineteenth Century. Oxford, Clarendon Press, 1948.

14.2.8.20   Usher, Abbott Payson, An Introduction to the Industrial History of England. Boston, Houghton Mifflin, 1920.

14.2.9   Economics and Economic Policy.

14.2.9.1   Hancock, William Keith, Wealth of Colonies. Cambridge, University Press, 1950.

74

14.2.10   Geography, Geopolitics and Regional Planning.

14.2.10.1   MacKinder, Sir Halford J., Britain and the British Seas.
               New York, Appleton, 1902.

14.2.14   Specific Peoples, Areas and Problems.

14.2.14.1   Vanderschmidt, Fred, What the English Think of Us. New
               York, McBride, 1948.

14.2.21   Miscellaneous

14.2.21.1   Williams, Ralph Vaughan, National Music. London, Oxford,
               University Press, 1934.

14.3	EUROPE GENERAL
14.3.1	Some General Bibliographies and Surveys.
14.3.1.1	U. S. Economic Cooperation Administration, Country Data Book. Washington, D. C., Government Printing Office, March, 1950. 16 vols. Economic data for all countries participating in O.E.E.C.
14.3.2	General Works on Nationalism.
14.3.2.1	Aris, R., "Nationalism and Europe," Contemporary Review, Vol. 158, Nov. 1940, pp. 537-543.
14.3.2.2	Benda, Julian, Discours a la Nation Européenne. Paris, 1933.
14.3.2.3	Coser, L. A., "Europe's Neurotic Nationalism; Tribalism Replaces Freedom and the Rights of Man," Commentary, Vol. 1, June 1946, pp. 58-63.
14.3.2.4	Dorpalen, A., "New Nationalism in Europe," Virginia Quarterly Review, Vol. 20, No. 3, July 1944, pp. 335-349.
14.3.3	Political Science.
14.3.3.1	Bingham, Alfred M., The United States of Europe. New York, Duell, 1940.
14.3.3.2	Brinton, Crane, The Temper of Western Europe. Cambridge, Harvard University Press, 1953.
14.3.3.3	Common Council for American Unity, European Beliefs Regarding the United States. New York, 1949.
14.3.3.4	Firsoff, V. A., The Unity of Europe: Realities and Aspirations. London, Drummond, 1947.
14.3.3.5	Friedrich, Carl J., "European Unity and the European Tradition," Confluence, Vol. II, No. 3, 1953, pp. 43-53.
14.3.3.6	Guerard Albert L., Europe Free and United. Stanford, Stanford University Press, 1945.
14.3.3.7	Harrison, George, Central Union of Europe. New York, McBridge, 1944.
14.3.3.8	- - - and P. Jordan, Central Union. London, British-Continental Syndicate, 1943.
14.3.3.9	Library of Congress, European Affairs Division, The European Press Today. Washington, D. C., 1949.
14.3.3.10	Mowat, R. B., "Europe's Need for a New Political Philosophy," Hibbert Journal, Vol. 34, April 1936, pp. 331-340.
14.3.3.11	Neumann, Sigmund, "Trends Toward Statism in Western Europe," Proceedings of the Academy of Political Science, May, 1950.

14.3.3.11a   Northrop, F. S. C., European Union and United States
Foreign Policy: A Study in Sociological Jurisprudence.
New York, Macmillan, 1954.

14.3.3.12   Pell, H., "Nationalism in Europe; an Economic Unit, Cultur-
ally Divided," Vital Speeches, Vol. 955, May 15, 1943, pp.
470-471.

14.3.3.13   Philip André, "La Crise Doctrinale du Socialisme en Europe,"
Revue Socialiste, April, 1952.

14.3.3.12   Tritsch, Walter, Europa und die Nationen. Darmstadt, Genf,
Holle Verlag, 1953.

14.3.5   Cultural Anthropology, Sociology and Social Psychology.

14.3.5.1   Demiashkevitch, Michael John, The National Mind: English,
French, German. New York, American Book Co., 1938.

14.3.5.2   Siegfried, André,"La Psychologie des Latins," Revue de
Psychologie des Peuples, May 1946, pp. 13-22.

14.3.5.3   - - - "La Psychologie des Relations Anglo-Allemandes,"
Revue de Psychologie des Peuples, 1952.

14.3.6   Linguistics, Sociology and Politics of Languages and Scripts.

14.3.6.1   Dauzat, A. L., Europe Linguistique. Paris, Biblothéque
Scientifique, 1940.

14.3.6.2   Deutsch, Karl W., "The Trend of European Nationalism -
The Language Aspect," American Political Science Review,
Vol. 36, No. 3, June 1942, pp. 533-541.

14.3.6.3   Dorpalen, A., "Language Question in Europe," South Atlantic
Quarterly, Vol. 41, April 1942, pp. 151-160. Revised, Free
World, Vol. 2, May 1942, pp. 356-359.

14.3.6.4   Meillet, A., Les langues dans l'Europe nouvelle. Paris,
Payot & Cie, 1928.

14.3.6.5   Rundle, S., Language as a Social and Political Factor in
Europe. London, Faber and Faber, 1944.

14.3.7   History, General.

14.3.7.1   Chadwick, Hector M., The Nationalities of Europe and the
Growth of National Ideologies. Cambridge, University Press,
1945.

14.3.7.2   Europe und der Nationalismus. Bericht über das III Internationale Historikertreffen in Speyer, Oct. 1949; Baden-
Baden, Verlag für Kunst und Wissenschaft, 1950.

14.3.7.3   Fay, Sidney B., "Union for Western Europe," Current
History, Vol. 16, No. 91, March 1949, pp. 156-161.

14.3.7.3a   Goriely, Georges, "Esquisse pour une histoire

de l'evolution du sentiment national en Europe," Cahiers Socialistes, No. 29, Brussells, 1951.

14.3.7.4   Huizinga, Jan, Patriotisme en nationalisme in de Europeesche geschiedenis tot het einde der 19e eeuw. Haarlem, 1940.

14.3.7.5   - - - Wachstum und Formen des Nationalen Bewusstseins in Europa bis zum Ende desig Jahrhunderts. 1942.

14.3.7.6   Philips, W. Alison, The Confederation of Europe: A Study of the European Alliance, 1813-1823, as an Experiment in the International Organization of Peace, 2nd Ed. London, Longmans, Green, 1920.

14.3.7.7   Pirenne, Henri, Mohammed and Charlemagne. New York, Norton, 1939.

14.3.7.8   Pouthas, Charles H., Le Mouvement des Nationalités en Europe dans la premiere moitie du XIX siecle. Paris, Centre de Documentation Universitaire, 1945.

14.3.7.9   Reau, Louis, L'Europe Française au Siècle des Lumières. Paris, Michel, 1938.

14.3.7.10   Rosenstock-Huessy, Eugen, Die Europaeischen Revolutionen. Jena, Diederichs, 1931.

14.3.8   Economic History

14.3.8.1   Birnie, Arthur, An Economic History of Europe, 1760-1930. New York, McVeagh, 1930.

14.3.8.2   Bowden, W., M. Karpovich and A. P. Usher, An Economic History of Europe since 1750. New York, American Book Co., 1937.

14.3.8.3   Cambridge Economic History of Europe, etc., Vol. I: The Agrarian Life of the Middle Ages. Cambridge, University Press, 1941.

14.3.8.4   Clapham, J. H., Economic Development of France and Germany, 1815-1914, 4th Ed. Cambridge, University Press, 1936.

14.3.8.5   Clough, S. B., and Charles W. Cole, Economic History of Europe, Rev. Ed. Boston, Heath, 1947.

14.3.8.6   Dopsch, A., The Economic and Social Foundations of European Civilization. London, K. Paul, Trench, Trubner, 1937.

14.3.8.7   Feis, Herbert, Europe, the World's Banker: An Account of European Foreign Investment and the Connection of World Finance with Diplomacy before the War. New Haven, Yale University Press, 1930.

14.3.8.8   Haliczer, Josef, "The Population of Europe, 1720, 1820,

1930," Geography, Vol. 19, No. 106, Dec. 1934, pp. 261-273.

14.3.8.9   Heaton, Herbert, Economic History of Europe, Rev. Ed.
New York, Harper, 1948.

14.3.8.10   Kulischer, Eugen M., Europe on the Move: War and Population Changes, 1917-1947. New York, Columbia University
Press, 1948.

14.3.8.11   Mantoux, Etienne, The Carthaginian Peace, or, The Economic
Consequences of Mr. Keynes. New York, Oxford University
Press, 1946.

14.3.8.12   Nussbaum, F. L., A History of the Economic Institutions of
Modern Europe. New York, Crofts, 1933.

14.3.8.13   Pirenne, Henri, Economic and Social History of Medieval
Europe. New York, Harcourt, Brace, 1937.

14.3.8.14   Schechtman, Joseph, European Population Transfers 1939-
1945. New York, Oxford University Press, 1946.

14.3.8.15   Thompson, James W., Economic and Social History of the
Middle Ages, 300-1300. New York, Century, 1928.

14.3.8.16   - - - Economic and Social History of Europe in the Later
Middle Ages, 1300-1500. New York, Century, 1931.

14.3.8.17   - - - The Literacy of the Laity in the Middle Ages. Berkeley,
University of California Press, 1939.

14.3.9   Economics and Economic Policy.

14.3.9.1   Balbus, "National Sovereignty and Industry: A Step Towards
the New Order in Europe," Fortnightly Review, Vol. 154
(New Series Vol. 148), Dec. 1940, pp. 541-547.

14.3.9.2   Delaisi, Francis, Le deux Europes: Europe industrielle
et Europe agricole, (Preface de Dannie Heinemann). Paris,
Payot, 1929.

14.3.9.3   - - - Die Revolution der Europaischen Wirtschaft. Stuttgart,
Berlin, Deutsche Verlagsanstalt, 1943.

14.3.9.4   Harris, Seymour E., The European Recovery Program.
Cambridge, Harvard University Press, 1948.

14.3.9.5   Hawtrey, E. G., Western European Union: Implications
for the United Kingdom. London, Royal Institute of International Affairs, 1949.

14.3.9.6   Studders, Herbert, Zur Integration der europäischen Arbeits-
kraft: Bevölkerungs - und arbeitsstatistische Unterlagen.
Frankfurt-am-Main, Lutzeyer, 1952.

14.3.10   Geography, Geopolitics and Regional Planning

14.3.10.1   Bogardus, J. F., Europe: A Geographical Survey. New York,
Harper, 1934.

14.3.10.2   Partsch, Joseph, Central Europe. New York, Appleton, 1903.

14.3.10.3   East, Gordon, An Historical Geography of Europe. New Dutton, 1935.

14.3.11   Biology; Genetics; Race.

14.3.11.1   Coon, Carleton Stevens, The Races of Europe. New York, Macmillan, 1939.

14.4   GERMANY AND GERMAN AUSTRIA

14.4.1   Some General Bibliographies.

14.4.1.1   Grothe, H., Grothe's Kleines Handwörterbuch des Grenz-
              und Auslands-Deutschtums. Berlin, Oldenbourg, 1932.

14.4.2   General Works on Nationalism (see also Section 14.4.7 below).

14.4.2.1   Andrews, R. C., "Nazi Prophet and Philosopher, Erwin
              Guido Kolbenheyer," Hibbert Journal, Vol. 43, Oct. 1944,
              pp. 21-28.

14.4.2.2   Hertz, F., "Fichte and Nationality," Contemporary Review,
              Vol. 163, April 1943, pp. 233-238.

14.4.3   Political Science.

14.4.3.1   Brady, Robert, Spirit and Structure of German Fascism.
              New York, Viking Press, 1937.

14.4.3.2   Ebenstein, William, The German Record: A Political
              Portrait. New York, Farrar and Rinehart, 1945.

14.4.3.3   Feder, Gottfried, Hitler's Official Programme and Its
              Fundamental Ideas. London, Allen and Unwin, 1934.

14.4.3.4   Fraenkel, Ernst, The Dual State. New York, Oxford Univer-
              sity Press, 1940. Stresses the existence of areas of legal
              predictability side by side with areas of extreme arbitrari-
              ness within the Nazi system.

14.4.3.5   Grossack, Martin, "A Study of Attitudes Toward American
              Policy in Germany," Public Opinion Quarterly, Vol. 16,
              1952, pp. 440-442.

14.4.3.6   Heiden, Konrad, History of National Socialism. New York,
              Knopf, 1935.

14.4.3.7   Hitler, Adolf, Mein Kampf. New York, Reynal and Hitchcock,
              1939.

14.4.3.8   Knight, Maxwell E., The German Executive: 1890-1933.
              Stanford, Stanford University Press, 1952.

14.4.3.9   Kohn, H., "Mass-Man Hitler," Atlantic Monthly, Vol. 173,
              April 1944, pp. 101-104.

14.4.3.10   Lerner, Daniel, and others, The Nazi Elite. Stanford,
              Stanford University Press, 1951.

14.4.3.11   Lundin, C. Leonard, "Nazification of Baltic German
              Minorities," Journal of Central European Affairs, Vol. 7,
              1947, pp. 1-28.

14.4.3.12   - - - "The Road from Tsar to Kaiser: Changing Loyalties
              of the Baltic Germans, 1905-1914," Journal of Central
              European Affairs, Vol. 10, No. 3, Oct. 1950, pp. 223-255.

14.4.3.13   Massing, Paul W., Rehearsal for Destruction: A Study of Political Anti-Semitism in Imperial Germany. New York, Harper, 1949.

14.4.3.14   Mellen, Sydney L. W., "The German People and the Post-war World, A Study Based on Election Statistics 1871-1933," American Political Science Review, Vol. 38, No. 4, Aug. 1943, pp. 601-625.

14.4.3.15   Neumann, Franz, Behemoth: The Structure and Practice of National Socialism. New York, Oxford University Press, 1942. The standard work on national socialism.

14.4.3.16   Roeseler, H., "Staat, Volk, Reich," Deutsche Rundschau, Vol. 265, Dec. 1940, pp. 105-108.

14.4.3.17   Schuman, Frederick L., The Nazi Dictatorship: Social Pathology and the Politics of Fascism, 2nd Rev. Ed. New York, Knopf, 1936.

14.4.3.18   Spengler, Oswald, Preussentum und Sozialismus. Munich, Beck, 1922.

14.4.3.19   Wheeler-Bennett, J. W., The Nemesis of Power: The German Army in Politics, 1918-1945. New York, St. Martin's Press, 1954.

14.4.5   Cultural Antrhopology, Sociology and Social Psychology.

14.4.5.1   Abel, Theodore F., Why Hitler Came Into Power. New York, Prentice-Hall, 1938.

14.4.5.2   Erickson, Erik H., "Hitler's Imagery and German Youth," Psychiatry, Journal of Biology and Pathology of Inter-personal Relations, Vol. 5, No. 4, 1942, pp. 475-493. Reprinted in Clyde Kluckhohn and H. A. Murray, Personality in Nature, Society and Culture, pp. 485-510.

14.4.5.3   Gilbert, G. M., A Nuremberg Diary. New York, Farrar, Strauss, 1947. A psychiatrist's comments on the Nazi defendants at the Nuremberg trials.

14.4.5.4   Kecskemeti, Paul and Nathan Leites, "Some Psychological Hypotheses on Nazi Germany," Journal of Social Psychology, Vol. 26, 1947, pp. 141-183; Vol. 27, 1948, pp. 91-117; Vol. 28, 1948, pp. 141-164.

14.4.5.5   Kracauer, Siegfried, From Caligari to Hitler: A Psycho-logical History of the German Film. Princeton, Princeton University Press, 1951.

14.4.5.6   Lewin, Herbert S., "Hitler Youth and the Boy Scouts of America: A Comparison of Aims," Human Relations, Vol. 1, 1947, pp. 206-227.

14.4.5.7   Loomis, C. P., "Political and Occupational Cleavages in a Hanoverian Village, Germany," Sociometry, Vol. 9, New York, Beacon House, 1946, pp. 316-333.

82

14.4.5.8   Lowie, Robert H., The German People: A Social Portrait
              to 1914. New York, Toronto, Farrar and Rinehart, 1945.

14.4.5.9   - - - Toward Understanding Germany. Chicago, University
              of Chicago Press, 1954.

14.4.5.10   Schaffner, Bertram, Father Land: A Study of Authoritar-
              ianism in the German Family. New York, Columbia Univer-
              sity Press, 1948.

14.4.5.11   Shils, Edward A., and Morris Janowitz, "Cohesion and
              Disintegration in the Wehrmacht in World War II," Public
              Opinion Quarterly, Vol. 12, Summer 1948, pp. 280-315.

14.4.5.12   Snyder, Louis L., "Nationalistic Aspects of the Grimm
              Brothers' Fairy Tales," The Journal of Social Psychology,
              Vol. 33, 1951, pp. 209-223.

14.4.5.13   Waehler, M., Der deutsche Volkscharakter. Jena, Diederichs,
              1937.

14.4.6   Linguistics and Sociology and Politics of Languages and Scripts.

14.4.6.1   Behaghel, Otto, Geschichte der Deutschen Sprache, 5th Ed.
              Berlin, Leipzig, DeGruyter, 1928.

14.4.6.2   Gassen, K., Die niederdeutsche Bewegung der Gegenwart.
              Greifswald, Bamberg, 1933.

14.4.6.3   Meyer, Gustav Friedrich, Unsere plattdeutsche Muttersprache.
              Garding, Luehr & Dircks, 1921.

14.4.7   History, General.

14.4.7.1   Anderson, Eugene N., Nationalism and the Cultural Crisis
              in Prussia, 1806-1815. New York, Farrar and Rinehart,
              1939.

14.4.7.2   Anrich, E., "War Stein Romantiker?" Historische Zeitschrift,
              Vol. 153, No. 2, 1936, pp. 290-305.

14.4.7.3   Aufricht, H., "J. G. Fichte und die Gessellschaftswissenschaften,"
              Zeitschrift für Offentliches Recht, Vol. 15, No. 3.

14.4.7.4   Barraclough, G., The Origins of Modern Germany. London,
              Oxford University Press, 1947.

14.4.7.5   Berlin, Universität, Friedrich Meinecke Institut, Das
              Hauptstadt-Problem in der Geschichte. Jahrbuch für
              Geschichte des Deutschen Ostens, Band I, Tübingen,
              Niemayer, 1952.

14.4.7.6   Eyck, Erich, Bismarck. Zurich, Rentsch, 1943. 3 vols.

14.4.7.7   - - - Bismarck and the German Empire. London, Allen
              and Unwin, 1950.

14.4.7.8   Fay, Sidney B., The Rise of Brandenburg-Prussia to 1786.
              New York, Holt, 1937.

14.4.7.9   Frings, T., et al., Kulturraeume und Kulturstroemungen im Mitteldeutschen Osten. Halle, Niemayer, 1936.

14.4.7.10   Henderson, Ernest F., A Short History of Germany. New York, Macmillan, 1940.

14.4.7.11   Joachimsen, P., Vom deutschen Volk zum deutschen Staat. Leipzig, Teubner, 1920.

14.4.7.12   Johansen, Paul, "Deutsch und Undeutsch im Mittelalterlichen Reval," Volksforschung, Vol. 3, No. 1, May 1939, pp. 41-50.

14.4.7.13   Kaufman, F. W., "Fichte and National Socialism," The American Political Science Review, Vol. 36, No. 3, June 1942, pp. 460-470.

14.4.7.14   Kohn, Hans, ed., German History: Some New German Views. Boston, Beacon Press, 1954.

14.4.7.15   - - - "Arndt and the Character of German Nationalism," American Historical Review, Vol. 54, No. 4, July 1949, pp. 787-803.

14.4.7.16   - - - "The Eve of German Nationalism," Journal of the History of Ideas, Vol. 12, No. 2, April 1951, pp. 256-286.

14.4.7.17   - - - "Father John's Nationalism," Review of Politics, Vol. 40, No. 4, Oct. 1949, pp. 419-432.

14.4.7.18   - - - "Paradox of Fichte's Nationalism," Journal of the History of Ideas, Vol. 10, No. 3, June 1949, pp. 319-343.

14.4.7.19   - - - "Romanticism and the Rise of German Nationalism," Review of Politics, Vol. 12, Oct. 1950, pp. 443-472.

14.4.7.20   - - - "Treitschke: Nationalism's Prophet," Review of Politics, Vol. 72, Oct. 1945, pp. 418-440.

14.4.7.21   Lamprecht, Karl, Deutsche Geschichte, Vol. 1, Berlin, Weidmann, 1920-1922. "Geschichte der Formen des Nationalbewusstseins," pp. 3-56.

14.4.7.22   Lerch, Eugen, Das Wort "Deutsch" Sein Ursprung und seine Geschichte bis auf Goethe. Frankfurt-am-Main, Vittorio Klostermann, 1941.

14.4.7.23   Lutz, Ralph H., ed., The Causes of the German Collapse in 1918. Stanford, Stanford University Press, 1934.

14.4.7.24   Mehring, Franz, Zur deutschen Geschichte. Leipzig, Soziologische Verlagsanstalt, 1931.

14.4.7.25   - - - Zur preussischen Geschichte vom Mittelalter bis Jena. Berlin, Soziologische Verlagsanstalt, 1930.

14.4.7.26   - - - Zur preussischen Geschichte von Tilsit bis zur Reichsgruendung. Berlin, Soziologische Verlagsanstalt, 1930.

14.4.7.27   Meynen, Emil, Deutschland und deutsches Reich: Sprachgebrauch und Begriffswesenheit des Wortes Deutschland.

84

Leipzig, Brockhaus, 1935.

14.4.7.28   Paul G., <u>Rassen und Raumgeschichte des deutschen Volkes.</u>
Munich, Lehmann, 1936.

14.4.7.29   Rosenberg, Arthur, <u>Geschichte der Deutschen Republik.</u>
Karlsbad, Graphia, 1935.

14.4.7.30   Simon, Walter M., "Variations in Nationalism During the
Great Reform Period in Prussia," <u>American Historical</u>
<u>Review,</u> Vol. 59, No. 2, Jan. 1954, pp. 305-321.

14.4.7.31   Snyder, Louis L., <u>From Bismarck to Hitler: The Background</u>
<u>of Modern German Nationalism.</u> Williamsport, Pa., Bayard
Press, 1935.

14.4.7.32   - - - <u>German Nationalism: The Tragedy of a People.</u>
Harrisburg, Stackpole, 1952.

14.4.7.33   Steefel, L. D., <u>The Schleswig-Holstein Question.</u> Cambridge,
Harvard University Press, 1932.

14.4.7.34   Thomas, R. Hinton, <u>Liberalism, Nationalism and the German</u>
<u>Intellectuals, 1822-1947.</u> Cambridge, Heffer, 1951.

14.4.7.35   Ulrich, Paul, <u>Studien zur Geschichte des deutschen National-</u>
<u>bewusstseins im Zeitalter des Humanismus und der Reforma-</u>
<u>tion.</u> (Hist. Studien hrsg. v. Ebering 298.) Berlin, 1936.

14.4.7.36   Weisgerber, J. Leo, <u>Der Sinn des Wortes 'Deutsch'.</u>
Göttingen, Vandenhoeck & Ruprecht, 1949.

14.4.8   Economic History.

14.4.8.1   Adler, Georg, <u>Epochen deutscher Handwerker-Politik.</u> Jena,
Fischer, 1903.

14.4.8.2   Gradmann, Robert, <u>Die staedtischen Siedlungen des Koenig-</u>
<u>greichs Wuertemberg.</u> Stuttgart, Engelhorn, 1914.

14.4.8.3   Helmreich, Ernst C., "Prussian Economic Policy," <u>Current</u>
<u>History,</u> Vol. 16, No. 91, March 1949, pp. 151-155.

14.4.8.4   Henderson, W. O., <u>The Zollverein.</u> Cambridge, University
Press, 1939.

14.4.8.5   Hildebrand, Christian, <u>Der Einbruch des Wirtschaftsgeistes</u>
<u>in das deutsche Nationalbewusstsein zwischen 1815 und 1871:</u>
<u>Der Anteil der Wirtschaft an der Reichsgründung von 1871.</u>
Drebkau N. L. Erich Leuschner, 1936.

14.4.8.6   Keyser, E., <u>Bevoelkerungsgeschichte Deutschlands.</u> Leipzig,
Hirzel, 1938.

14.4.8.7   Shotwell, James T., <u>What Germany Forgot.</u> New York,
Macmillan, 1940.

14.4.8.8   Sombart, Werner, <u>Die deutsche Volkswirtschaft im neun-</u>
<u>zehnten Jahrhundert.</u> Berlin, Bondi, 1921.

14.4.8.9   Stolper, Gustav, The German Economy, 1870-1940: Issues and Trends. New York, Reynal and Hitchcock, 1940.

14.4.8.10   Thompson, James W., Feudal Germany. Chicago, University of Chicago Press, 1928.

14.4.8.11   Veblen, Thorstein, Imperial Germany and the Industrial Revolution. New York, Viking, 1939.

14.4.8.12   Wildmann, Hans, Geschichte des Buchhandels vom Altertum bis zur Gegenwart. Wiesbaden, Otto Harrassowitz, 1952.

14.4.10   Geography, Geopolitics and Regional Planning.

14.4.10.1   Luedtke, Gerhard, and Lutz Mackensen, Deutscher Kulturatlas. Berlin, Walter de Gruyter, 1928-1936. 5 vols. Important.

14.4.10.2   Whittlesey, Derwent, German Strategy of World Conquest. New York, Farrar and Rinehart, 1942.

14.4.14   Specific Peoples, Areas and Problems.

14.4.14.1   Norman, Albert, Our German Policy: Propaganda and Culture. New York, Vantage Press, 1951.

14.5	THE AUSTRO-HUNGARIAN EMPIRE AND THE DANUBIAN AREA
14.5.1	General Bibliographies and Surveys.
14.5.1.1	Demorgny, Gustave, Danube et Adriatique. Paris, 1933.
14.5.1.2	Lehmann, John, Down River: A Danubian Study. London, Cresset Press, 1939.
14.5.1.3	Lengyel, Emil, The Danube. New York, Random, 1939.
14.5.3	Political Science.
14.5.3.1	Borsody, Stephen, ed., Liberation and Union: The Future of Danubian Federation and the Atlantic Union. Washington, Freedom and Union, 1952. A Symposium by Paul Auer and others. Letter from Iron Curtainland.
14.5.3.2	Chamberlain, Joseph P., The Regime of the International Rivers: Danube and Rhine. New York, Columbia University, 1923. Columbia University Studies in History, Economics and Public Law, Vol. 105, No. 1 (Whole No. 327).
14.5.3.2a	Deutsch, Karl W., "Problems and Prospects of Federation," in Cyril E. Black, ed., Challenge in Eastern Europe, New Brunswick, N.J., Rutgers University Press, 1954, pp. 219-244
14.5.3.3	Fisher, Helen, "Cross-Currents in Danubian Europe," Foreign Policy Reports, Vol. 13, July 15, 1937, pp. 102-112.
14.5.3.4	France, Ministère des Affaires Étrangères, Notes sur la Question Danubienne. 1933.
14.5.3.5	Gestetner, Leo, The Danubian Case. London, Allen and Unwin, 1941.
14.5.3.6	Gedye, G. E. R., Fallen Bastions: The Central European Tragedy. London, Gollancz, 1939.
14.5.3.7	Great Britain, Central Office of Information, Reference Division, International Control of the Danube. London, Nov. 11, 1947.
14.5.3.8	Great Britain, Parliament House of Commons Library, International Control of the Danube. London, Dec. 18, 1946.
14.5.3.9	Gross, Feliks, Crossroads of Two Continents: A Democratic Federation of East-Central Europe. New York, Columbia University Press, 1945.
14.5.3.10	Gyorgy, Andrew, "Danubian Federation," Thought, Vol. 23, New York, March 1948, pp. 36-58.
14.5.3.11	Hantos, Elmer, Die Neuordnung des Donauraumes. Berlin, Heymann, 1935.
14.5.3.12	Hanun, M. Theodore Y., A Plan of the Central European Federation. Caldwell, Idaho, Caxton, 1949.

14.5.3.13   Hertz, Friedrich O., "Danubian Union," Contemporary Review, Vol. 157, London, March 1940, pp. 284-290.

14.5.3.14   Hodža, Milan, Federation in Central Europe. London, Jarrolds, 1942.

14.5.3.15   Jászi, Oskar, "Danubia, Old and New," Proceedings of the American Philosophical Society for Promoting Useful Knowledge, Vol. 93, April 18, 1949, pp. 1-31.

14.5.3.16   - - - "Future of Danubia," Journal of Central European Affairs, Vol. 1, July 1941, pp. 127-147.

14.5.3.17   - - - "Neglected Aspects of the Danubian Drama," Slavonic Review, Vol. 14, July 1935, pp. 53-67.

14.5.3.18   Kolnai, Aurel, "Austria and the Danubian Nations," Journal of Central European Affairs, Vol. 3, July 1943, Jan. 1944, pp. 167-182, 441-462.

14.5.3.19   - - - "Danubia: A Survey of Plans of Solution," Journal of Central European Affairs, Vol. 3, Jan. 1944, pp. 441-462.

14.5.3.20   Lang, R. D., "Central Europe and European Unity," Journal of Central European Affairs, Vol. 6, April 1946, pp. 21-29.

14.5.3.21   Macartney, C. A., Hungary and Her Successors: The Treaty of Trianon and its Consequences, 1919-1937. London, Oxford University Press, 1937.

14.5.3.22   - - - Problems of the Danube Basin. Cambridge, University Press, 1942.

14.5.3.23   Plutynski, Antoni, We Are 115 Millions, trans. H. C. Stevens. London, Eyre and Spottiswoode, 1944.

14.5.3.24   Rossetti, Carlo, Il Danubio, Fiume Internazionale. Milano, Institute per gli studi di politica internazionale, 1937.

14.5.3.25   Stanczyk, Jan, "Social War: Federation of Central Europe," Free World, Vol. 1, Jan. 1942, pp. 359-361.

14.5.3.26   Strasburger, Henryk, The Core of a Continent: Problems of Central and Eastern Europe. Philadelphia, American Academy of Political and Social Science, 1943.

14.5.3.27   Taylor, A. J. P., "National Independence and the 'Austrian Idea': Difficulty of Securing National Amalgamation in the New National States," Political Quarterly, Vol. 16, July 1945, pp. 234-246.

14.5.3.28   Traisner, K., "Key Position of Europe; Need of a Danubian Federation," Catholic World, Vol. 154, Oct. 1941, pp. 37-45.

14.5.3.29   Vambery, R., "United States of the Danube," The Nation, Vol. 149, Dec. 23, 1939, pp. 705-707.

14.5.3.30   Ward, B., "Ignaz Seipel and the Anschluss," Dublin Review, Vol. 203, July 1938, pp. 33-50.

14.5.5   Cultural Anthropology, Sociology and Social Psychology.

14.5.5.1   Roucek, Joseph S., "The Sociological Weaknesses of Federation Plans for Central-Eastern Europe," Journal of Legal and Political Sociology, Oct. 1943, pp. 94-116.

14.5.7   History, General.

14.5.7.1   Commission Europeénne du Danube, La Commission Europeénne du Danube et son Oeuvre de 1856 a 1931. Paris, Imp. nationale, 1931.

14.5.7.2   - - - Dix ans de Régime international sur le Danube fluviale 1920-1930. Wien, Spies, 1931.

14.5.7.3   Gulick, Charles A., Austria from Hapsburg to Hitler. Berkeley, University of California Press, 1948. 2 vols.

14.5.7.4   Jaszi, Oscar, The Dissolution of the Hapsburg Monarchy. Chicago, University of Chicago Press, 1929. P.

14.5.7.5   Kann, Robert A., The Multinational Empire: Nationalism and National Reform in the Hapsburg Monarchy, 1848-1918. New York, Columbia University Press, 1950. 2 vols.

14.5.7.6   Kogan, A. G. "Social Democrats and the Conflict of Nationalities in the Hapsburg Monarchy," Journal of Modern History, Vol. 21, Sept. 1949, pp. 204-217.

14.5.7.7   Kohn, Hans, "The Legacy of the Hapsburgs," in Hans Kohn's Not By Arms Alone, Harvard University Press, 1940, pp. 43-64.

14.5.7.8   Mitrany, David, The Effect of the War in South-Eastern Europe. New Haven, Yale University Press, 1936.

14.5.7.9   Schneefuss, Walter, Donäuraume und Donaureiche. Wien-Leipzig, Braumüller, 1944.

14.5.7.10   Somogyi, Joseph de, "The Historical Development of the Danubian Problem to the Present," Journal of Central European Affairs, Vol. 8, April 1948, pp. 45-57.

14.5.7.11   Zarek, Otto, A History of Hungary. London, Selwyn & Blount, 1939.

14.5.8   Economic History.

14.5.8.1   Gratz, Gustav, ed., Der wirtschaftliche Zusammenbruch Oesterreich-Ungarns: Die Tragoedie der Erschoepfung. Vienna, Hoelder-Pichler-Tempsky A. -G., 1930.

14.5.8.2   - - - and Rich. Schueller, Die aeussere Wirtschaftspolitik Oesterreich-Ungarns: Mittelerropaeische Plaenc. Vienna, Hoelder-Pichler-Tempsky A. -G., 1925.

14.5.8.3   Grossman, Henryk, Oesterreich's Handelspolitik mit Bezug auf Galizien in der Reformperiode 1772-1790. Vienna, Konegen, 1914.

14.5.8.4   Hertz, Friedrich C., The Economic Problem of the Danubian States: A Study in Economic Nationalism. London, Gollancz, 1947.

14.5.8.5   Niederle, Miroslav, L'Evolution et l'et Actuel de la Collaboration Économique dans le Bassin du Danube. Prague, Orbis, 1938.

14.5.8.6   Poniatowski, Jozef, "Population of the Intermarium after the Second World War," The Eastern Quarterly, Vol. 4, No. 3, London, July, 1951.

14.5.9   Economics and Economic Policy.

14.5.9.1   Basch, Antonin, The Danube Basin and the German Economic Sphere. New York, Columbia University Press, 1943.

14.5.9.2   Karlikovitch, Douchan, Le Rapprochement Économique des Pays Danubiens. Paris, 1937.

14.5.9.3   Pasvolski, Leo, Economic Nationalism of the Danubian States. New York, Macmillan, 1938.

14.5.10   Geography, Geopolitics and Regional Plannning.

14.5.10.1   Kiss, George, The Danube Basin: Patterns in Political Geography. Ann Arbor, 1945 (1 roll of microfilm).

14.5.10.2   - - - "'TVA' On the Danube," The Geographical Review, Vol. 37, No. 2, 1947, pp. 274-302.

14.5.10.3   Popper, Otto, "The International Regime of the Danube" (with discussion), Geographical Journal, Vol. 102, Nov., Dec. 1943, pp. 240-253.

14.5.10.4   Roucek, Joseph S.,"The Geopolitics of Danubia," World Affairs, Vol. 17, Oct. 1946, pp. 316-322.

14.5.10.5   Tibal, Andre, Les Communications dans l'Europe Danubienne. Paris, Publications de la Conciliation, 1933.

14.5.14   Specific Peoples, Areas and Problems.

14.5.14.1   Schacher, Gerhard, Central Europe and the Western World. London, Allen and Unwin, 1936.

14.6	THE SLAVIC WORLD, THE BALKANS AND BALTIC COUNTRIES, AND THE USSR
14.6.1	General Bibliographies and Surveys.
14.6.1.1	Adamic Louis, My Native Land. New York, Harper, 1943.
14.6.1.2	Buell, Raymond L., Poland: Key to Europe. New York, Knopf, 1939.
14.6.1.3	Chamberlin, William H., Soviet Russia. Boston, Little, Brown, 1931.
14.6.1.4	- - - The Ukraine: A Submerged Nation. New York, Macmillan, 1944.
14.6.1.5	Epstein, F. T., "A Short Bibliography on the Slaves," The Slavonic and East European Review, Vol. 22, No. 60, Oct. 1944, pp. 110-119.
14.6.1.6	Kerner, Robert J., ed., Czechoslovakia, Twenty Years of Independence. Berkeley, Los Angeles, University of California Press, 1940.
14.6.1.7	Kridl, Manfred, Wladyslaw Malinowsky and Jozef Wittlin, eds., For Your Freedom and Ours. New York, Ungar, 1943.
14.6.1.8	Royal Institute of International Affairs, Information Dept., South-Eastern Europe: A Political and Economic Survey. London, 1939.
14.6.1.9	Sweet-Escott, Bickham, Greece, A Political and Economic Survey, 1939-1953. New York, Royal Institute of International Affairs, 1954.
14.6.1.10	Zoltowski, Adam, Border of Europe, A Study of the Polish Easten Provinces. London, 1950.
14.6.2	General Works on Nationalism.
14.6.2.1	Cermelj, Lavo, Life-and-Death Struggle of a National Minority. Ljubljana, 1930.
14.6.2.2	Karpovitch, M., "Vladimir Soloviev on Nationalism," Review of Politics, Vol. 8, April 1946, pp. 183-191.
14.6.2.3	Kohn, Hans, Nationalism in the Soviet Union. New York Columbia University Press, 1933.
14.6.2.4	Lamont, Corliss, The Peoples of the Soviet Union. New York, Harcourt, Brace, 1946.
14.6.2.5	Shumeyko, Stephen, Ukranian National Movement. New York, United Ukrainian Organizations of the U.S., 1939.
14.6.2.6	Symonolewicz, F., "The Studies in Nationality and Nationalism in Poland between the Two Wars, 1918-1939," Bulletin of the Polish Institute of Arts and Sciences in America, Vol. 2,

14.6.3   Political Science.

14.6.3.1   Barghoorn, Frederick C., The Soviet Image of the United
                States: A Study in Distortion. New York. Harcourt, Brace,
                1950.

14.6.3.2   Barghoorn, Frederick C., Soviet Russian Nationalism.
                New York, Oxford U.P., 1956.

14.6.3.3   Barker, Elizabeth, Macedonia: Its Place in Balkan Power
                Politics. London, Royal Institute of International Affairs,
                1950.

14.6.3.4   Bassow, Whitman, "Izvestia Looks Inside U.S.A.," Public
                Opinion Quarterly, Vol. 12, 1948, pp. 430-439.

14.6.3.5   Beneš, Edvard, Bohemia's Case for Independence. London,
                Allen and Unwin, 1912.

14.6.3.6   - - - Future of the Small Nations and the Idea of Federation.
                New York, Czechoslovakia Information Service, 1942.

14.6.3.7   - - - Nová Slovanská Politika. Prague, V. Zikes, 1946.

14.6.3.8   - - - Ou vont les Slaves? Úvahy o slovanství (Essais sur
                le slavisme). Paris, Ed. de Notre Temps, 1948.

14.6.3.9   - - - The Problem of the Small Nations after the World War
                (Reprinted from the Slavonic Review). London School of
                Slavonic Studies in the University of London, 1926.

14.6.3.10   - - - The World Crisis, Continuity of Law and New Revolu-
                tionary Law. New York, Czechoslovak Government Informa-
                tion Service, 1945.

14.6.3.11   Berman, Harold Joseph, Justice in Russia: An Interpretation
                of Soviet Law. Cambridge, Harvard University Press, 1950.

14.6.3.12   Black, Cyril E., ed., Challenge in Eastern Europe. New
                Brunswick, Rutgers University Press, 1954.

14.6.3.13   Brailsford, H. N., Macedonia: Its Races and Their Future.
                London, Methuen U. Co., 1906.

14.6.3.14   Brumberg, A., "Soviet Campaign Against Survivals of
                Capitalism," Russian Review, Vol. 12, April 1953, pp. 65-78.

14.6.3.15   Fainsod, Merle, How Russia Is Ruled. Cambridge, Harvard
                University Press, 1953.

14.6.3.16   Fischel, Alfred, Der Panslavismus bis zum Weltkrieg.
                Stuttgart, Gotta, 1919. P.

14.6.3.17   Geshkoff, Theodore I., Balkan Union: A Road to Peace in
                Southeastern Europe. New York, Columbia University Press,
                1940.

14.6.3.18   Inkeles, Alex, Public Opinion in Soviet Russia. Cambridge,
                Harvard University Press, 1950.

92

14.6.3.19   Kohn, Hans, "The Historical Roots of Czech Democracy," in Czechoslovakia, ed. by Robert J. Kerner, University of California Press, 1940, pp. 91-105.

14.6.3.20   Masaryk, T. G., The Making of a State. New York, Stokes, 1927.

14.6.3.21   - - - The New Europe. London, Eyre and Spottiswoode, 1918.

14.6.3.22   Padelford, Norman J., Peace in the Balkans: The Movement Towards International Organization in the Balkans. New York, Oxford University Press, 1935.

14.6.3.23   Pap, M., "Soviet Difficulties in the Ukraine," Review of Politics, Vol. 14, April 1952, pp. 204-232.

14.6.3.24   Papanace, Constantin, Pro Balcania: Considerations sur l' Union Balkenique et la Solution des Problemes Litigieux de ce Secteur Europeén. Roma, 'Armatolii,' 1951.

14.6.3.25   Peev, Konstantin J., Balkanpakt und Balkanbund. Sofia, Staikoff, 1937.

14.6.3.26   Renner, Karl, Das nationale und das oekonomische problem der Tschechoslowakei. Prague, Verlag der Deutschen Sozialdemokratischen Arbeiterpartei, 1926.

14.6.3.27   Ripka, Hubert, Munich: Before and After. London, Gollancz, 1939.

14.6.3.28   Rostow, Walt Whitman, The Dynamics of Soviet Society. New York, Norton, 1954.

14.6.3.29   Schlesinger, Rudolf, Federalism in Central and Eastern Europe. London, Kegan Paul, 1945.

14.6.3.30   Schuman, Frederick L., Soviet Politics at Home and Abroad. New York, Knopf, 1946.

14.6.3.31   Seton-Watson, Hugh, The East European Revolution. London, Methuen, 1934.

14.6.3.32   Stavrianos, Leften S., Balkan Federation: A History of the Movement Toward Balkan Unity in Modern Times. Northampton, Dept. of History of Smith College, 1944.

14.6.3.33   Towster, Julian, Political Power in the U.S.S.R., 1917-1947: The Theory and Structure of Government in the Soviet State. New York, Oxford University Press, 1948.

14.6.3.34   - - - "Soviet Federation; How the Soviets Solved the Problems of Nationalism," Current History, New Series Vol. 16, No. 91, March 1949, pp. 131-135.

14.6.3.35   Wendel, Herrmann, Makedonien und der Friede. München, Musarion Verlag, 1919.

14.6.3.36   Zinner, Paul E., "Marxism in Action: The Seizure of Power in Czechoslovakia," Foreign Affairs, Vol. 28, 1950, pp. 644-658.

14.6.5   Cultural Anthropology, Sociology and Social Psychology.

14.6.5.1   Gorer, Geoffrey and John Rickman, The People of Great Russia: A Psychological Study. New York, Chanticleer Press, 1950.

14.6.5.2   Mead, Margaret, Soviet Attitudes Toward Authority: An Inter-Disciplinary Approach to Problems of Soviet Character. New York, McGraw-Hill, 1952.

14.6.5.3   - - - "A Natural History Approach to Soviet Character," Natural History Magazine, September 1951, pp. 296-303 and p. 336.

14.6.5.4   Rauchberg, Heinrich, Der nationale Besitzstand in Boehmen. Leipzig, Duncker and Humblot, 1905. 2 vols.

14.6.5.5   Schlesinger, Rudolf, ed., The Family in the U.S.S.R.: Documents and Readings. London, Routledge and Kegan Paul, 1949.

14.6.5.6   Tomasic, Dinko, Personality and Culture in Eastern European Politics. New York, Stewart, 1948.

14.6.6   Linguistics and Sociology and Politics of Languages and Scripts.

14.6.6.1   Entwistle, W. J. and W. A. Morison, Russian and the Slavonic Languages. London, Faber and Faber, 1949.

14.6.6.2   Ilarion, Mitropolit, History of Ukrainian Literary Language (in Ukrainian). Winnipeg, 1950.

14.6.6.3   Mladenov, Stefan, Geschichte der Bulgarischen Sprache. Berlin, Leipzig, De Gruyter, 1929.

14.6.6.4   Weingart, Miloš, et al., Slovanské spisovné jazyky v době přítomne. Prague, 1937.

14.6.7   History, General.

14.6.7.1   Allen, W. E. C., The Ukraine: A History. Cambridge, University Press, 1940.

14.6.7.2   Anastasoff, Christ, The Tragic Peninsula: A History of the Macedonian Movement for Independence since 1878. St. Louis, Blackwell, Weilandy, 1938.

14.6.7.3   Aufricht, Hans, Adamantios Koraes and the Image of the Modern Greek State. New York, New Europe, Inc., 1942.

14.6.7.4   Beneš, Edvard, Světová válka a naše revoluce, vzpomínky a úvahy z bojů za svobodu naroda. Prague, Orbis, 1935. 3 vols.

14.6.7.5   Carr, Edward Hallett, A History of Soviet Russia, The Bolshevik Revolution, 1917-1923. 3 vols. London, Macmillan, 1950, esp. I, 410-428; III, 549-566.

14.6.7.6   Chaconas, Stephen G., Adamantios Korais: A Study in Greek Nationalism. New York, Columbia, 1942.

14.6.7.7   Heymann, Egon, Balkan: Kriege, Bundnisse, Revolutionen;
            150 Jahre Politik und Schicksaal. Berlin, Junker and
            Dunnhaupt, 1938.

14.6.7.8   Hrushevsky, Michael A., History of Ukraine. New Haven,
            Yale University Press, 1941.

14.6.7.9   Jurgela, C. R., History of the Lithuanian Nation. New York,
            The Lithuanian-American Information Center, 1948.

14.6.7.10   Karpovich, Michael M., Imperial Russia 1801-1917. New
            York, Holt, 1932.

14.6.7.11   Kohn, Hans, "Dostoievsky's Nationalism," Journal of the
            History of Ideas, Vol. 6, No. 4, Oct. 1945, pp. 385-414.

14.6.7.12   - - - "The Heritage of Masaryk," The Annals of the American
            Association of Political and Social Sciences, Vol. 258, July
            1949, pp. 70-74.

14.6.7.13   - - - Pan-Slavism: Its History and Ideology. South Bend,
            University of Notre Dame Press, 1953.

14.6.7.14   - - - "The Permanent Mission: An Essay on Russia,"
            Review of Politics, Vol. 10, No. 3, July 1948, pp. 267-289.

14.6.7.15   Maschke, Erich, Das Erwachen des Nationalbewusstseins
            im deutschslawischen Grenzraum. Leipzig, 1933.

14.6.7.16   Petrovich, M. B., "Ludovit Stur and Russian Panslavism,"
            Journal of Central European Affairs, Vol. 12, April 1952,
            pp. 1-19.

14.6.7.17   Schevill, Ferdinand, The History of the Balkan Peninsula,
            From the Earliest Times to the Present Day. New York,
            Harcourt, Brace, 1933.

14.6.7.18   Seton-Watson, Hugh, Eastern Europe between the Wars.
            Cambridge, University Press, 1945.

14.6.7.19   - - - and Robert William, A History of the Czechs and
            Slovaks. London, Hutchinson, 1943.

14.6.7.20   - - - and - - - A History of the Roumanians from Roman
            Times to the Completion of Unity. Cambridge,

14.6.8.21   Shuster, G. N., "Masaryk," Commonweal, Vol. 26, Oct. 22,
            1937, pp. 593-594.

14.6.7.22   Skendi, S., "Beginnings of Albanian Nationalist Trends in
            Culture and Education 1878-1912," Journal of Central
            European Affairs, Vol. 12, Jan. 1953, pp. 356-367.

14.6.7.23   Vernadsky, George, A History of Russia. New Haven, Yale
            University Press, 1948.

14.6.7.24   Wiskeman, Elizabeth, Czechs and Germans. London, Oxford
            University Press, 1938.

14.6.8   Economic History

14.6.8.1   Baykov, Alexander, The Development of the Soviet Economic
                System: An Essay on the Experience of Planning in the USSR.
                Cambridge, University Press, 1947.

14.6.8.2   Rašin, Alois, Financial Policy of Czechoslovakia during the
                First Year of Its History. London, New York, Milford, 1923.

14.6.8.3   Wilhelm, Warren, "Soviet Central Asia: Development of a
                Backward Area," Foreign Policy Reports, Vol. 25, No. 18,

14.6.8.4   Wszelaki, Jan, "The Rise of Industrial Middle Europe,"
                Foreign Affairs, Oct. 1951, pp. 124-134.

14.6.9   Economics and Economic Policy.

14.6.9.1   Carrie, R. Albrecht, "Fiume: Nationalism Versus Economics,"
                Journal of Central European Affairs, Vol. 2, April 1942,
                pp. 49-63.

14.6.9.2   Vucinich, Alexander, Soviet Economic Institutions: The
                Social Structure of Production Units. Stanford, Stanford
                University Press, 1952.

14.6.10   Geography, Geopolitics and Regional Planning.

14.6.10.1   Cressey, George B., The Basis of Soviet Strength. New York,
                Whittlesey, McGraw-Hill, 1945.

14.6.10.2   Kerner, Robert H., The Urge to the Sea: The Course of
                Russian History: The Role of Rivers, Portages, Ostrogs,
                Monasteries, and Furs. Berkeley, University of California
                Press, 1942.

14.7	FRANCE
14.7.2	General Works on Nationalism.
14.7.2.1	Corrigan, B., "Charles Maurras: Philosopher of Nationalism," Queens Quarterly, Vol. 52, No. 3, Aug. 1945, pp. 288-298.
14.7.2.2	Hayes, Carlton, France: A Nation of Patriots. New York, Columbia University Press, 1930. P.
14.7.3	Political Science
14.7.3.1	Blum, Leon, For All Mankind. New York, Viking, 1946. Discusses requirements for a national leading class, holding that the French middle class no longer fulfills them.
14.7.3.2	Padover, Saul, French Institutions: Values and Politics. Stanford, Stanford University Press, 1954.
14.7.3.3	Pickles, Dorothy, French Politics: The First Years of the Fourth Republic. New York, Royal Institute of International Affairs, 1953.
14.7.3.4	Sforza, C., "Fear Across the Borders," Current History, Vol. 44, July 1936, pp. 39-42.
14.7.3.5	Thomson, David, Democracy in France: The Third and Fourth Republics, 2nd Ed. New York, Oxford University Press, 1952.
14.7.3.6	Wambaugh, Sarah, The Saar Plebiscite. Cambridge, Harvard University Press.
14.7.5	Cultural Anthropology, Sociology and Social Psychology.
14.7.5.1	Metraux, Rhoda and Margaret Mead, Themes in French Culture. Stanford, Stanford University Press, 1954.
14.7.5.2	Rogoff, Natalie, "Social Stratification in France and in the United States," American Journal of Sociology, Jan. 1953.
14.7.6	Linguistics and Sociology and Politics of Language and Scripts.
14.7.6.1	Cohen, Marcel, Histoire d'une Langue: le Français, des Lointaines Origines à Nos Jours. Paris, Editions hier et aujour a'hui, 1947.
14.7.6.2	Pansier, P., Histoire de la Langue Provençale à Avignon, du 12me au 19me Siècle. Aignon, Aubanel frères, 1927. 4 vols.
14.7.6.3	Wartburg, Walther von, Evolution et Structure de la Langue Francaise. Leipzig, Verlin, Teubner, 1934.
14.7.7.	History General.
14.7.7.1	Brinton, Crane, A Decade of Revolution, 1789-1799. New York, London, Harper, 1934.
14.7.7.2	Deutsch, Harold C., The Genesis of Napoleonic Imperialism. Cambridge, Harvard University Press; London, Humphrey

Cambridge, Harvard University Press; London, Humphrey Milford, 1938.

14.7.7.3　　Dupre, H., "Carnot's Nationalism," South Atlantic Quarterly, Vol. 37, July 1938, pp. 291-306.

14.7.7.4　　Greer, D. M. The Incidence of the Emigration During the French Revolution. Cambridge, Harvard University Press, 1951.

14.7.7.5　　Headings, M. J., "French Freemasonry under the Third Republic (Nationalism and Internationalism)," Johns Hopkins University Studies in Historical and Political Science, Vol. 66, No. 1, 1949, pp. 104-151.

14.7.7.6　　Kämpf, Hellmut, Pierre Dubois und die geistigen Grundlagen des franzöisischen Nationalbewusstseins um 1300. (Beiträge zur Kulturgesch. d. Mittelalters und der Renaissance 54.) Leipzig, Berlin, 1935.

14.7.7.7　　Kohn, H., "Madame de Stael: Liberal and Nationalist," Forum, Vol. 111, Feb. 1949, pp. 81-85.

14.7.7.8　　Meyer, Herbert, Die Oriflamme und das französische Nationalgefühl. Nachrichten d. Ges. d. Wissenschaften zu Göttingen. Philol. - hist. Klasse, 1930.

14.7.7.9　　Seignobos, Charles, A History of the French People. London, Cape, 1933.

14.7.8　　Economic History.

14.7.8.1　　Clough, S. B., France: A History of National Economics, 1789-1939. New York, Scribners, 1939.

14.7.8.2　　Landes, David S., "French Entrepreneurship and Industrial Growth in the Nineteenth Century," Journal of Economic History, Vol. 9, No. 1, May 1949, pp. 45-61.

14.7.11　　Biology; Genetics; Race.

14.7.11.1　　Biermann, B., "Racism in France," Commonweal, Vol. 28, Aug. 12, 1938, pp. 402-403. Discussion Vol. 28, Sept. 9, 23, 1938, pp. 502-556.

14.7.14　　Specific Peoples, Areas and Problems.

14.7.14.1　　Rose, Arnold M., "Anti-Americanism in France," Antioch Review, Winter 1952-1953.

14.8	BELGIUM AND THE NETHERLANDS
14.8.1	General Bibliographies and Surveys.
14.8.1.1	Goris, Jan-Albert, ed., Belgium. Berkeley, University of California Press, 1946.
14.8.6	Linguistics, Sociology and Politics of Languages and Scripts.
14.8.6.1	Hellinga, Wytze, De Opbouw van de Algemeen Beschaafde Uitspraak van het Nederlands, Amsterdam. N.V. Noord-Hollandsche Uitgeversmaatschappij, 1938.
14.8.6.2	Kloeke, G. G., De Hollandsche Expansie in de 16de en 17de eeuw en haar weerspiegeling in de hedendaagsche Nederlandsche dialecten. The Hage, Nijhoff, 1927.
14.8.6.3	Lecoutere, Charles P., and L. Grootaers, Inleiding tot de Taalkunde en tot de Geschiedenis van het Nederlandsch, 6th Ed. Leuven, Vlaamsche Drukkerij, 1941.
14.8.6.4	Perre, A. van de, The Language Question in Belgium. London, Richards, 1919.
14.8.7	History, General.
14.8.7.1	Geyl, P., Eenheid en Tweeheid in de Nederlanden. Lochen De Tijdstroom, 1946.
14.8.7.2	- - - Geschiedenis van de Nederlansche Stam. Encyclopaedie van de Wereldbibliotheek, 1930-1937. 5 vols.
14.8.7.3	- - - De Groot Nederlandsche Gedachte. Haarlem, H. D. Tjeenk Willink, 1925.
14.8.7.4	- - - "Language and Nationality in the Low Countries - A Correction," History, Sept. 1946, pp. 137-139.
14.8.7.5	Hoogewerff, G. J., "Uit de Geschiedenis van het Nederlandsch Nationaal Besef," Tijdschrift voor Geschiedenis, No. 2, 1929.
14.8.7.6	Huizinga, J., Verzamelde Werken, Vol. 2. Haarlem, H. D. Tjeenk Willink & Zoon, 1948, pp. 95-556. Various essays on the origins of Dutch Nationality.
14.8.7.7	Pirenne, Henri, Belgian Democracy. Manchester 1915, London 1915 (written 1910).
14.8.7.8	- - - Medieval Cities. Princeton, Princeton University Press, 1946.
14.8.7.9	Renier, G. J., The Criterion of Dutch Nationhood. London, Allen and Unwin, 1946.
14.8.7.10	- - - The Dutch Nation: An Historical Study. London, Allen and Unwin, 1944.

14.8.7.11 Romein, Jan en Annie, De Lage Landen Bij de Zee:
      Geillustreerde Geschiedenis van het Nederlandse Volk.
      Utrecht, Uitgeversmaatschappij, W. De Haann V., 1949.

14.8.7.12 Vlekke, Bernhard H. M., Evolution of the Dutch Nation.
      New York, Roy, 1945.

14.8.8   Economic History.

14.8.8.1   Baasch, Ernst, Hollaendische Wirtschaftsgeschichte. Jena,
      Gustav Fischer, 1927.

14.9   SCANDINAVIA, INCLUDING FINLAND AND ICELAND

14.9.1   General Bibliographies and Surveys.

14.9.1.1 Anderson, B., The Northern Countries. Published by the
Foreign Ministries of Denmark, Finland, Iceland, Norway
and Sweden. Uppsula, Almquist and Wiksell, 1951.

14.9.1.2 Koht, Halvdan and Sigmund Skard, The Voice of Norway.
New York, Columbia University Press, 1944.

14.9.6   Linguistics and Sociology and Politics of Languages and Scripts.

14.9.6.1 Setälä, E. N., La lutte des langues en Finlande. Paris, Libe,
Champion, 1920.

14.9.6.2 Sommerfelt, A., The Written and Spoken Word in Norway.
Oxford, 1942.

14.9.6.3 - - - "Conditions de la Formation d'une Langue Commune,"
Actes du quatrième Congrès International de Linguistes,
(1936), Copenhagen, Munksgaard, 1938, pp. 42-48.

14.9.7   History, General.

14.9.7.1 Hovde, Brynjolf, The Scandinavian Countries, 1720-1865:
The Rise of the Middle Classes. Boston, Chapman and
Grimes, 1943. 2 vols.

14.9.7.2 Larsen, Karin, A History of Norway. Princeton, Princeton
University Press, 1948.

14.9.7.3 Lindgren, R. E., The Dissolution of the Swedish-Norwegian
Union. Center for Research and World Political Institutions,
Princeton University, Princeton, 1952. (Unpublished.)

14.9.8   Economic History.

14.9.8.1 Thomas, Dorothy Swaine, Social and Economic Aspects of
Swedish Population Movements 1750-1933. New York,
Macmillan, 1941.

14.9.9   Economics and Economic Policy.

14.9.9.1 Delegation for the promotion of Economic Cooperation between
the Northern Countries, The Northern Countries in World
Economy: Denmark, Finland, Iceland, Norway, Sweden.
Kopenhagen, Levin and Munksgaard, 1937.

14.9.9.2 Fleetwood, E. E., Sweden's Capital Imports and Exports.
Stockholm, Natur Och Kultur, 1947.

14.9.14   Specific Peoples, Areas and Problems.

14.9.14.1 Scott, Franklin D., The United States and Scandinavia.
Cambridge, Harvard University Press, 1950.

14.10	SWITZERLAND
14.10.1	General Bibliographies and Surveys.
14.10.1.1	Brosi, I., Die Schweiz und der Irredentismus.Eine Historisch-politische Darstellung. Basel, Brodbeck-Frehner, 1935.
14.10.3	Political Science.
14.10.3.1	Cramer, Frederick H., "Switzerland: Federalism Triumphant," Current History, Vol. 6, No. 91, March 1949,
14.10.5	Cultural Anthropology, Sociology and Social Psychology.
14.10.5.1	Weilenmann, Hermann, Pax Helvetica. Erlenbach-Zurich, Eugen Rentsch Verlag, 1951.
14.10.5.2	- - - Uri, Land, Volk, Staat Wirtschaft & Kultur. Erlenbach-Zurich, Eugen Rentsch Verlag, 1943.
14.10.6	Linguistics and Sociology and Politics of Languages and Scripts.
14.10.6.1	Henry, R., La Suisse et la Question des Langues. Bern, Staempfli, 1915.
14.10.6.2	Schmid, Karl, "Fuer unser Schweizerdeutsch," in Die Schweiz: Ein nationales Jahrbuch, 1936. Zurich, Neue Helvetische Gesellschaft, 1936.
14.10.6.3	Schuerch, Ernst, Sprachpolitische Erinnerungen. Bern, Verlag Paul Haupt, 1943.
14.10.6.4	Weilenmann, Hermann, Die vielsprachige Schweiz. Eine Lösung des Nationalitätenproblems. Basel, Rheinverlag, 1925. P.
14.10.7	History, General.
14.10.7.1	Englert-Faye, Curt, Vom Mythus zur Idee der Schweiz. Zurich, Atlantic-Verlag, 1940.
14.10.7.2	Nabholz, Hans, Geschichte der Schweiz. Zurich, Schulthess, 1932-1938. 2 vols.
14.10.7.3	Weilenmann, Hermann, Der Zusammenschluss zur Eidgenossenschaft. Zurich, Büchergilde Gutenberg, 1940.
14.10.8	Economic History.
14.10.8.1	Bickel, W., Bevölkerungsgeschichte und Bevölkerungspolitik der Schweiz seit dem Ausgang des Mittelalters. Zurich, Gutenberg, 1947.

14.11	ITALY
14.11.3	Political Science.
14.11.3.1	Ascoli, Max and Arthur Feiler, Fascism for Whom? New York, Norton, 1938.
14.11.3.2	Goetz, Walter, "Die Enstehung der Italienischen Nationalitat," and "Das Werden des Italienischen Nationalgefuhls," in Italien im Mittelalter, Leipzig, Koehler and Amelang, 1942, pp. 16-124.
14.11.3.3	Mussolini, Benito, The Doctrine of Fascism, trans. by E. Cops, 2nd Ed. Firenze, Vallecchi, 1937.
14.11.3.4	Salvemini, Gaetano, Under the Axe of Fascism. New York, Viking, 1936.
14.11.3.5	- - - and George LaPiana, What to Do with Italy. New York, Duell, Sloan and Pearce, 1943.
14.11.3.6	Schmidt, C. T., The Corporate State in Action. New York, Oxford University Press, 1939.
14.11.3.7	- - - The Plough and the Sword: Labor, Land, and Property in Fascist Italy. New York, Columbia University Press, 1938.
14.11.6	Linguistics, Sociology and Politics of Languages and Scripts.
14.11.6.1	Bertoni, Guilio, Storia della Lingua Italiana. Rome Lib. Castellani, 1934.
14.11.6.2	Hall, Robert A., The Italian Questione della Lingua: An Interpretative Essay. Chapel Hill, University of North Carolina Press, 1942.
14.11.6.3	Von Wartburg, Walter, Die Entstehung der romanischen Volker. 2nd ed., Tuebingen, Niemeyer, 1951.
14.11.6.4	- - - , La posizione della lingua Italiana nel mondo Neolatino. Leipzig, Keller, 1936.
14.11.7	History, General.
14.11.7.1	Noether, Emiliana Pasca, Seeds of Italian Nationalism 1700-1815. New York, Columbia University Press, 1951.
14.11.7.2	Olschki, Leonardo, The Genius of Italy. New York, Oxford University Press, 1949.
14.11.8	Economic History.
14.11.8.1	Doren, Alfred, Italienische Wirtschaftsgeschichte. Jena, Fischer, 1934.
14.11.14	Specific Peoples, Areas and Problems.
14.11.14.1	Hughes, H. Stuart, The United States and Italy. Cambridge, Harvard University Press, 1953.

14.12	SPAIN, PORTUGAL AND LATIN AMERICA
14.12.1	General Bibliographies and Surveys.
14.12.1.1	Butland, Gilbert J., Chile, An Outline of its Geography, Economics and Politics, Rev. Ed. New York, Royal Institute of International Affairs, 1953.
14.12.1.2	Camacho, J. A., Brazil: An Interim Assessment. New York, Royal Institute of International Affairs, 1952.
14.12.1.3	Galbraith, W. O., Colombia: A General Survey. New York, Royal Institute of International Affairs, 1953.
14.12.1.4	Linke, Lilo, Ecuador: Country of Contrasts. New York, Royal Institute of International Affairs, 1954.
14.12.1.5	Osborne, Harold, Bolivia: A Land Divided. New York, Royal Institute of International Affairs, 1954.
14.12.1.6	Pendle, George, Paraguay: A Riverside Nation. New York, Royal Institute of International Affairs, 1954.
14.12.1.7	- - - , Uruguay: South America's First Welfare State. New York, Royal Institute of International Affairs, 1952.
14.12.3	Political Science.
14.12.3.1	Mariategui, José Carlos, Siete Ensayes de Interpretación de la Realidad Peruana. Lima Biblioteca "Amanta," 1944.
14.12.3.2	Ortega y Gasset, Jose, Invertebrate Spain. New York, Norton, 1937.
14.12.3.3.	Perón, Juan Domingo, El Pueblo Quiere Saber de que se Trata, Buenos Aires, N.P., 1944.
14.12.3.4	United States, Department of State, Blue Book on Argentina: Consultation among the American Republics with Respect to The Argentina Situation. Memorandum of the United States Government, Washington, D. C., February, 1946. New York, Greenberg, 1946.
14.12.5	Cultural Anthropology, Sociology and Social Psychology.
14.12.5.1	Metraux, Rhoda, "Some Aspects of Hierarchical Structure in Haiti," in S. Tax, Ed., Acculturation in the Americas, Vol. 2, Proceedings of the 29th International Congress of Americanists, University of Chicago Press, 1952.
14.12.5.2	Michels, Roberto, "Das Problem der Structuraenderung in einigen Suedeamerikanischen Staaten, insbesondere Argentinien und Brasilien, zumal im Hinblick auf den Italienischen Einfluss," Weltwirtschaftliches Archiv, Jena, Vol. 34, 1931, II, pp. 565-597.
14.12.6	Linguistics, Sociology and Politics of Languages and Scripts.
14.12.6.1	Entwistle, W. J., The Spanish Language, together with

Portuguese, Catalan and Basque. London, Faber and Faber, 1936.

14.12.6.2 Menéndez-Pidal, Ramón, Castilla, la tradición, el idioma. Buenos Aires, Espasa-Calpe Argentina, 1945.

14.12.7 History, General.

14.12.7.1 Bushnell, David, "The 'Recent Indian' in Guatemala 1800 to 1880," in Delaware Notes, Twenty-Fifth Series, University of Delaware, 1952, pp. 35-54.

14.12.7.2 Coester, Alfred L., The Literary History of Spanish America. New York, Macmillan, 1941.

14.12.7.3 Marti, José, The America of José Marti: Selected Writings. New York, Noonday Press, 1953.

14.12.7.4 Rennie, Ysabel F., The Argentina Republic. New York, Macmillan, 1945.

14.12.7.5 Rippy, J. Fred, Historical Evolution of Hispanic America, 3rd Ed. New York, Crofts, 1945.

14.12.7.6 Verissimo, Erico, Brazilian Literature; An Outline. New York, Macmillan, 1945.

14.12.8 Economic History.

14.12.8.1 Bonn, Moritz J., Spanien's Niedergang waehrend der Preisrevolution des 16. Jahrhunderts. Stuttgart, Cotta, 1896.

14.12.8.2 Jenks, Leland H., Our Cuban Colony: A Study in Sugar. New York, Vanguard Press, 1928.

14.12.8.3 Mosk, Sanford A., The Industrial Revolution in Mexico. Berkeley, University of California Press, 1950.

14.12.8.4 - - - "Pathology of Democracy in Latin America: An Economist's Point of View," American Political Science Review, Vol. 44, No. 1, March 1950, pp. 129-142.

14.12.8.5 Rippy, J. Fred, The Capitalists and Columbia. New York, Vanguard Press, 1931.

14.12.8.6 - - - Latin America and the Industrial Age, 2nd Ed. New York, Putnam, 1947.

14.12.8.7 Ruehl, Alfred, Vom Wirtschaftsgeist in Spanien. Leipzig, Quelle & Meyer, 1928.

14.12.8.8 Wythe, George, Industry in Latin America, 2nd Ed. New York, Columbia University Press, 1949.

14.12.9 Economics and Economic Policy.

14.12.9.1 Gordon, Wendell Chaffee, The Economy of Latin America. New York, Columbia University Press, 1950.

14.12.9.2 Harris, Seymour E., ed., Economic Problems of Latin America. New York, McGraw-Hill.

14.12.9.3 Soule, George P., David Efron and N. T. Ness, Latin America in the Future World. New York, Farrar and Rinehart, 1945.

14.12.10 Geography, Geopolitics and Regional Planning.

14.12.10.1 James, Preston E., Latin America. New York, Odyssey Press, 1942.

14.12.10.2 McBride, G. M., Chile: Land and Society. New York, American Geographical Society, 1936.

14.12.14 Specific Peoples, Areas and Problems.

14.12.14.1 Dickmann, Enrique, La Infilitración Nazi-Fascista en la Argentina. Buenos Aires, Ediciones Sociales Argentinas, 1939.

14.12.14.2 Padelford, Norman Judson, The Panama Canal in Peace and War. New York, Macmillan, 1942.

14.14   ASIA, GENERAL SURVEY

14.14.1   Some General Bibliographies and Surveys.

14.14.1.1   Katz-Suchy, Julius, "National Liberation and Social Pro-
             gress in Asia," Annals of the American Academy of
             Political and Social Science, Vol. 276, July 1951, pp. 48-59.

14.14.1.2   Lattimore, Owen D., The Situation in Asia. Boston, Little,
             Brown, 1949.

14.14.1.3   - - - Solution in Asia. Boston, Little, Brown, 1945.

14.14.2   General Works on Nationalism.

14.14.2.1   Cole, Allan B., Nationalism and Revolution in Asia. Part
             of this work is an analytical survey of recent changes in
             the area; was available in pre-publication in June 1952
             form through the American Friends Service Committee.

14.14.2.2   Emerson, Rupert, "Paradoxes of Asian Nationalism,"
             Far Eastern Quarterly, Vol. 13, No. 2, Feb. 1954, pp. 131-
             142.

14.14.2.2. a Holland, William L., ed., Asian Nationalism and the West:
             A Symposium Based on Documents and Reports of the
             Eleventh Conference of the Institute of Pacific Relations
             (George McT. Kahin, Philippe Devillers, T. H. Silcock
             and Ungou A. Aziz, contributors). New York, Macmillan,
             1953.

14.14.2.3   Roy, M. N., "Asian Nationalism," Yale Review, Vol. 42,
             No. 1, Sept., 1952, pp. 96-102.

14.14.2.4   Sen, B. R., "Nationalism and the Asian Awakening," Annals
             of the American Academy of Political and Social Science,
             Vol. 282, July 1952, pp. 108-113.

14.14.3   Political Science.

14.14.3.1   Rosinger, Lawrence K., The State of Asia: A Contemporary
             Survey. New York, Knopf, 1951.

14.14.8   Economic History.

14.14.8.1   Schechtman, Joseph B., Population Transfers in Asia.
             New York, Oxford University Press, 1949.

14.14.14   Specific Peoples, Areas and Problems.

14.14.14.1   Dallin, David J., The Rise of Russia in Asia. New Haven,
             Yale University Press, 1949.

14.15   NEAR EAST: INCLUDING NORTH AFRICA, THE ARAB WORLD, THE OTTOMAN EMPIRE AND ITS SUCCESSORS, IRAN AND AFGHANISTAN

14.15.1   General Bibliographies and Surveys.

14.15.1.1   Antonius, George, The Arab Awakening: The Story of the Arab National Movement. Philadelphia, Lippincott, 1939.

14.15.1.2   Gibb, H. A. R., The Arabs. Oxford, Clarendon Press, 1940.

14.15.1.3   Ireland, P. W., ed., The Near East. Chicago, University of Chicago Press, 1942.

14.15.1.4   Izzeddin, Nejla, The Arab World: Past, Present and Future. Chicago, Regnery, 1953.

14.15.1.5   Royal Institute of International Affairs, The Middle East, A Political and Economic Survey, Rev. Ed. New York, 1954.

14.15.1.6   Zischka, A., Die Auferstehung Arabiens. Leipzig, 1935.

14.15.2   General Works on Nationalism.

14.15.2.1   Anon, "Arab Nationalism in French North Africa: The Tunisian Disorders," Illustrated London News, Vol. 220, Feb. 9, 1952, p. 203.

14.15.2.2   - - - "Nationalism and the Trade Unions in French North Africa; Trade Unions and Nationalism in Tunisia," World Today, Vol. 8, June 1952, pp. 251-252.

14.15.2.3   Goitstein, S. D., "Cross-Currents in Arab National Feelings," Commentary, Vol. 7, Feb. 1949, pp. 156-161.

14.15.2.4   Heyd, Uriel, Foundations of Turkish Nationalism. London, Luzac, 1950.

14.15.2.5   Kohn, Hans, A History of Nationalism in the East. New York, Harcourt, Brace, 1929.

14.15.2.6   - - - Nationalism and Imperialism in the Hither East. New York, Harcourt, Brace, 1932.

14.15.2.7   - - - Western Civilization in the Near East. New York, Columbia University Press, 1936.

14.15.2.8   Luethy, H., trans. by M. J. Goldbloom, "Cross Tides of North African Revolt; A Firsthand Report on Algeria, Morocco, Tunisia," Commentary, Vol. 14, Nov. 1952, pp. 433-449.

14.15.2.9   MacCallum, Elizabeth P., The Arab Nationalist Movement. New York, Foreign Policy Association, 1935.

14.15.2.10   Marmorstein, E., "Fate of Arabdom: A Study in Comparative Nationalism," International Affairs, Vol. 25, Oct. 1949, pp. 475-491.

14.15.2.11   Middle East Institute, Nationalism in the Middle East.
              A series of addresses presented at the Sixth Annual
              Conference on Middle East Affairs, sponsored by the
              Middle East Institute, Washington, D. C., March 21-22,
              1952.

14.15.2.12   Rivlin, B., "The Tunisian Nationalist Movement: Four
              Decades of Evolution," Middle East Journal, Vol. 6, No. 2,
              1952, pp. 167-193.

14.15.2.13   - - - "Unity and Nationalism in Libya," The Middle East
              Journal, Vol. 3, Jan. 1949, pp. 31-54.

14.15.2.14   Wright, Esmond, "Egypt: Nationalism in Adolescence,"
              World Affairs, Vol. 4, No. 3, July 1950, pp. 335-349.

14.15.3   Political Science.

14.15.3.1   Alexander, M., "Near East's Communist-Fascist Front;
              and Ominous Alliance Against Israel and the West,"
              Commentary, Vol. 13, May 1952, pp. 456-462.

14.15.3.2   Atiyah, Edward, An Arab Tells His Story, A Study in
              Loyalties. London, Murray, 1946.

14.15.3.3   Hourani, A., "Decline of the West in the Middle East,"
              International Affairs, Vol. 29, Jan. 1953, pp. 22-42;
              April 1953, pp. 156-183.

14.15.3.4   Krout, John A., ed., International Tensions in the Middle
              East. New York, Academy of Political Science, Columbia
              University, 1952.

14.15.3.5   Ladgham, Bahi, "The Truth about Tunisia," The New
              Leader, June 8, 1953.

14.15.3.6   Laisay, Michel, Du Panarabisme a la Ligue Arabe. Paris,
              1948.

14.15.3.7   The Tunisian Office for National Liberation, An Account
              of the Tunisian Question and its Most Recent Developments.
              New York, 1952.

14.15.3.8   - - - Farhat Hached: Tunisian Labor Leader, Patriot,
              Martyr. New York, July 1953.

14.15.3.9   - - - The Tunisian Question: Economic Policy of the
              French Protectorate. New York, Oct. 1952.

14.15.3.10   - - - The Tunisian Question: Franco-Tunisian Relations.
              New York, April 1950-Dec. 1952.

14.15.3.11   Werth, A., "Murder in Tunis," New Statesman and Nation,
              Vol. 44, Dec. 13, 1952, pp. 711-712.

14.15.3.12   - - - "Tunisian Tangle," New Statesman and Nation,
              Vol. 44, July 19-26, 1952, p. 63, pp. 95-96.

14.15.3.13   Zafrulla Khan, Muhammed, Minister of Foreign Affairs and Commonwealth Relations, "Pakistan Mission to the United Nations," Speech on the Tunisian Question to the First Committee of the Eighth Session of the United Nations General Assembly on Oct. 23, 1953, PR 150-T.

14.15.5   Cultural Anthropology, Sociology and Social Psychology.

14.15.5.1   Lambton, A. K. S., Landlord and Peasant in Persia: A Study of Land Tenure and Land Revenue Administration. New York, Oxford University Press, 1953.

14.15.6   Linguistics, Sociology and Politics of Languages and Scripts.

14.15.6.1   Simon, Jean, "L'Aire et la Durée des Dialectes Coptes," Actes du quatrième Congrès International de Linguistes (1936), Copenhagen, E. Munksgaard, 1938, pp. 182-185.

14.15.7   History, General.

14.15.7.1   Brockelmann, Carl, History of the Islamic Peoples. New York, Putnam, 1947.

14.15.7.2   Dodwell, Henry, The Founder of Modern Egypt: A Study Muhammad 'Ali. Cambridge, University Press, 1931.

14.15.7.3   Hitti, Phillip K., The Arabs: A Short History. Princeton, Princeton University Press, 1943.

14.15.7.4   - - - A History of the Arabs. London, Macmillan, 1951.

14.15.7.5   - - - A History of Syria, Including Lebanon and Palestine. New York, Macmillan, 1951.

14.15.7.6   Lawrence, T. E., Seven Pillars of Wisdom. Garden City, Doubleday, 1938.

14.15.7.7   Longrigg, S. H., Iraq 1900-1950: A Political, Social and Economic History. New York, Oxford University Press, 1954.

14.15.8   Economic History.

14.15.8.1   Fogg, Walter, "Village, Tribal Markets, and Towns: Some Considerations Concerning Urban Development in the Spanish and International Zones of Morocco," The Sociological Review, Vol. 32, Nos. 1 and 2, Jan., April 1940, pp. 85-107.

14.15.8.2   Puryear, Vernon J., International Economics and Diplomacy in the Near East: A Study of British Commercial Policy in the Levant, 1834-1853. Stanford, Stanford University Press, 1935.

14.15.8.3   Ruehl, Alfred, Vom Wirtschaftsgeist in Orient. Leipzig, Quelle & Meyer, 1925.

14.15.9   Economics and Economic Policy.

14.15.9.1   Bonne, Alfred, The Economic Development of the Middle East: An Outline of Planned Reconstruction after the War. New York, Oxford University Press, 1945.

14.15.9.2   Issawi, Charles Philip, Egypt: An Economic and Social Analysis. London, New York, Oxford University Press, 1947.

14.15.9.3   Longrigg, S. H., Oil in the Middle East. New York, Oxford University Press, 1954.

14.15.10   Geography, Geopolitics and Regional Planning.

14.15.10.1   Van Valkenburg, Samuel, Whose Promised Lands? A Political Atlas of the Middle East and India. New York, Foreign Policy Association, 1946.

14.15.14   Specific Peoples, Areas and Problems.

14.15.14.1   Duhamel, G., "L'isolement de la France et la Problème Tunisien," France Illustration, Vol. 353, July 19, 1952, p. 54.

14.15.14.2   Fitzsimons, M. A., "Britain and the Middle East 1944-1950," Review of Politics, Vol. 13, Jan. 1951, pp. 21-28.

14.15.14.3   Royal Institute of International Affairs, Great Britain and Egypt 1914-1951. Information Paper No. 19, London, 1952.

14.16	INDIA, PAKISTAN AND CEYLON
14.16.1	General Bibliographies and Surveys.
14.16.1.1	Chani, A. R., Pakistan: A Select Bibliography. Lahore, Pakistan Association for the Advancement of Science, University Institute of Chemistry, 1951.
14.16.1.2	Government of India, Ministry of Education and Broadcasting, India: A Reference Manual. Delhi, 1953.
14.16.1.3	India Government Office, Census of India. 1951.
14.16.1.4	- - - Statistical Abstract, India 1949, Vol. 1, Office of the Economic Adviser. Government of India, Calcutta, 1950.
14.16.1.5	Thorner, Daniel, "Recent Books on India and Pakistan," in The Middle East Journal, Vol. 6, No. 1, Winter 1952, pp. 89-92.
14.16.2	General Works on Nationalism.
14.16.2.1	Brown, W. Norman, "India's Pakistan Issue," Proceedings of the American Philosophical Society, Vol. 91, No. 2, April 1947, pp. 162-180.
14.16.2.2	Duffett, W. E., India Today: The Background of the Indian Nationalist Movement. Toronto, 1941.
14.16.2.3	Park, Richard Leonard, The Rise of Militant Nationalism in Bengal: A Regional Study of Indian Nationalism. Ph.d. thesis, Harvard University, unpublished, 1951.
14.16.2.4	Symonds, Richard, The Making of Pakistan. London, Faber, 1950.
14.16.3	Political Science.
14.16.3.1	Ambedkar, Bhimrao Ramjo, States and Minorites, What are Their Rights and How to Secure Them in the Constitution of Free India. Bombay, Thacker, 1947.
14.16.3.2	Gandhi, M. E., His Own Story. London, Allen and Unwin, 1930.
14.16.3.3	Nehru, Jawaharlal, The Discovery of India. London, Meridian Books, 1947; New York, John Day, 1946.
14.16.3.4	- - - Nehru on Gandhi. New York, John Day, 1948.
14.16.3.5	- - - Toward Freedom: The Autobiography of Jawaharlal Nehru. New York, John Day, 1941.
14.16.3.6	- - - The Unity of India, Collected Writings 1937-1940. London, Drummond, 1941.
14.16.5	Cultural Anthropology, Sociology and Social Psychology.
14.16.5.1	Murphy, Gardner, In the Minds of Men: A Study of Human

Behavior and Social Tensions in India. New York, Basic Books, 1953.

14.16.5.2   Ram, Pars and Gardner Murphy, "Recent Investigations of Hindu-Moslem Relations in India," Human Organization, Vol. 1, No. 4, Spring 1952, pp. 13-16.

14.16.6   Linguistics, Sociology and Politics of Languages and Scripts.

14.16.6.1   Ahmad, A. Z., ed., National Language for India: A Symposium. Allahabad, Kitabistan, 1941.

14.16.6.2   Bansilal, Govindlal, The Constitution of India and the Indian Languages. Bombay 26, 14A, Bomanji Petit Road, Govindlal Bansilal, 1954.

14.16.6.3   Bomon-Behram, B. K., Educational Controversies in India: The Cultural Conquest of India under British Imperialism. Bombay, Taraporevala, 1943, p. 633.

14.16.6.4   Ceylon, Report of the Select Committee of the State Council on Sinhalese and Tamil as Official Languages. Colombo, Government Press, 1946.

14.16.6.5   Chatterji, Suniti Kumar, Languages and the Linguistic Problem, Oxford Pamphlets on Indian Affairs, No. 11, 2nd Ed. London, Oxford University Press, 1944.

14.16.6.6   - - - "The Languages of India," Indian News, Government of India Information Services, Washington, D. C., March 7, 1953.

14.16.6.7   Chib, Som Nath, Language, Universities and Nationalism in India. 1936.

14.16.6.8   Congress Central Publicity Board, Linguistic States. New Delhi, 1951. Campaign pamphlet for the 1952 general elections.

14.16.6.9   India, Census of India, Paper No. 1, 1954. Languages - 1951 Census. Delhi, Manager of Publications, 1954.

14.16.6.10   India. Linguistic Survey. Vols. 1-11. Calcutta, Superintendent of Government Printing, 1903-28. Compiled under the direction of Sir George A. Grierson. Summary and index of language names in Vol. 1 (1927).

14.16.6.11   India. Ministry of Education. A Review of Education in India during 1948-49, 1949-50, 1950-51, New Delhi. Government of India Press, 1949-51. 3 vols.

14.16.6.12   Mujeeb, M., "Indian Education" Retrospect and Prospect," Pacific Affairs, Vol. 26, Summer 1953, pp. 208-219.

14.16.6.13   Mukerdji, S. N., Education in India: Today and Tomorrow. Baroda, Acharya Book Depot, 1952.

14.16.6.14   Namboodripad, E. M. S., The National Question in Kerala. Bombay, People's Publishing House, 1952.

14.16.6.15   Rao, P. K., "Language Policy in Mysore Education," <u>Mysore Economic Review</u>, 39 (1), Jan. 1953, pp. 45-46.

14.16.6.16   Sharma, Rambilas, <u>The Question of an Obligatory State Language in India</u>. Bombay, People's Publishing House, 1954.

14.16.6.17   Weerawardana, I. D. S., "Minority Problems in Ceylon," <u>Pacific Affairs</u>, 25 (3), Sept. 1952, pp. 278-287.

14.16.6.18   Windmiller, Marshall, "Linguistic Regionalism in India," <u>Pacific Affairs</u>, Vol. 27, 1954, pp. 291-318.

14.16.7   History, General.

14.16.7.1   Gooneratne, Chandra, Dharma S., <u>The Development of Political Consciousness in India, 1757-1931</u>. Chicago, University of Chicago thesis, 1936; privately published.

14.16.7.2   McCully, Bruce Tiebout, <u>English Education and the Origins of Indian Nationalism</u>. New York, Columbia University Press, 1940.

14.16.7.3   Mookerji, Radakumud, <u>The Fundamental Unity of India.</u> London, Longmans Green, 1914.

14.16.8   Economic History.

14.16.8.1   Chandrasekhar, S., <u>India's Population: Fact and Policy,</u> Rev. Ed. New York, Asia Press (Augustus M. Kelley, Inc.), 1950.

14.16.8.2   Knight, Sir Henry, <u>Food Administration in India, 1939-1947.</u> Stanford, Stanford University Press, 195 .

14.16.8.3   Thorner, Daniel, <u>Investment in Empire: British Railway and Steam Shipping Enterprise in India 1825-1849.</u> Philadelphia, University of Pennsylvania Press, 1950.

14.16.8.4   Vakil, C. N., <u>Economic Consequences of Divided India: A Study of the Economy of India and Pakistan.</u> Bombay, Vora, 1950.

14.16.9   Economics and Economic Policy.

14.16.9.1   Davis, Kingsley, <u>The Population of India and Pakistan.</u> Princeton, Princeton University Press, 1951.

14.16.9.2   Gadgil, D. R., "The Economic Prospect for India," <u>Pacific Affairs,</u> Vol. 22, June 1949.

14.16.9.3   - - - "Problems of Rural Life," <u>Annals of the American Academy of Political and Social Science,</u> Vol. 244 (India Speaking), May 1944, pp. 84-91.

14.16.9.4   Thorner, Daniel, "Problems of Economic Development in India," <u>Annals of the American Academy of Political and Social Science,</u> Vol. 268, March 1950, pp. 96-103.

14.16.10   Geography, Geopolitics and Regional Planning.

14.16.10.1   India Government Office, India in Maps, issued by the Publication Division, Ministry of Information and Broadcasting. Government of India, Delhi, 1950.

14.16.14   Specific Peoples, Areas and Problems.

14.16.14.1   Brecher, M., The Struggle for Kashmir. New York, Oxford University Press, 1953.

14.17	SOUTHEAST ASIA: BURMA, MALAYA, THAILAND, INDO-CHINA AND INDONESIA
14.17.1	Some General Bibliographies.
14.17.1.1	Furnivall, John S., Colonial Policy and Practice: A Comparative Study of Burma and Netherlands India. Cambridge, University Press, 1948.
14.17.2	General Works on Nationalism.
14.17.2.0	Ellsbree, Willard H., Japan's Role in Southeast Asian Nationalist Movements, 1940-1945. Cambridge, Harvard University Press, 1953.
14.17.2.1	Emerson, Rupert, et al., Government and Nationalism in Southeast Asia. International Secretariat, Institute of Pacific Relations, 1942.
14.17.2.2	Kahin, George McTurnan, Nationalism and Revolution in Indonesia. Ithaca, Cornell University Press, 1952.
14.17.3	Political Science.
14.17.3.1	Donnison, F. S. V., Public Administration in Burma. New York, Royal Institute of International Affairs, 1953.
14.17.3.1a	Emerson, Rupert, Representative Government in Southeast Asia. Cambridge, Harvard, 1955.
14.17.3.2	Hammer, Ellen, The Struggle for Indo-China. Stanford, Stanford University Press, 195 .
14.17.3.3	Jones, S. W., Public Administration in Malaya. New York, Royal Institute of International Affairs, 1953.
14.17.3.4	Purcell, Victor, The Chinese in Southeast Asia. London, Oxford University Press, 1950.
14.17.5	Cultural Anthropology, Sociology and Social Psychology.
14.17.5.1	Benedict, Ruth, Thai Culture and Behavior. New York, 1943. Mimeographed.
14.17.5.2	Wertheim, W. F., Effects of Western Civilization on Indonesian Society. New York, International Secretariat, Institute of Pacific Relations, 1950.
14.17.6	Linguistics and Sociology and Politics of Languages and Scripts.
14.17.6.1	Alisjahbana, Takdir, "The Indonesian Language -- By-Product of Nationalism," Pacific Affairs, Vol. 22, No. 4, Dec. 1949, pp. 388-392.
14.17.14	Specific Peoples, Areas and Problems.
14.17.14.1	Emerson, Rupert, The Netherlands Indies and the United States. Boston, World Peace Foundation, 1942.

14.18   THE FAR EAST: CHINA, KOREA, JAPAN AND THE
            PHILIPPINES

14.18.1   Some General Bibliographies and Surveys.

14.18.1.1   Benedict, Ruth, The Chrysanthemum and the Sword: Pat-
            terns of Japanese Culture. Boston, Houghton Mifflin, 1945.

14.18.1.2   Lattimore, Owen, D., Pivot of Asia: Sinkiang and the Inter-
            Asian Frontiers of China and Russia. Boston, Little, Brown,
            1950.

14.18.1.3   Shen, Tsung-lien, Tibet and the Tibetans. Stanford, Stanford
            University Press, 1953.

14.18.2   General Works on Nationalism.

14.18.2.0   Bransby-William, M. E., "Nationalism in the Middle and
            Far East," Military Review, March 1954.

14.18.2.0a Brown, Delmer, Nationalism in Japan: An Introductory
            Historical Analysis. Berkeley, University of California
            Press, 1955.

14.18.2.1   Moran, James W., The Development of Chinese Nationalism,
            1912-1948, thesis, Ph.D. University of Colorado, unpublished.

14.18.3   Political Science.

14.18.3.0   Bell, W. Macmahon, Nationalism and Communism in East
            Asia. Melbourne, Melbourne University Press; New York,
            Cambridge University Press, 1953.

14.18.3.1   Butow, Robert J. C., Japan's Decision to Surrender, Stan-
            ford, Stanford University Press, 1954.

14.18.3.2   Lineberger, Paul M., The Political Doctrine of Sun Yat-Sen.
            Baltimore, Johns Hopkins, 1937.

14.18.3.3   North, Robert C., Kuomintang and Chinese Communist
            Elites. Stanford, Stanford University Press, 1952.

14.18.3.4   - - - Moscow and Chinese Communists. Stanford, Stanford
            University Press, 195 .

14.18.3.5   Rostow, Walt Whitman, et al., The Prospects for Chinese
            Communist China, Preliminary Ed. Cambridge-New York,
            Massachusetts Institute of Technology Press and Wiley,
            1954.

14.18.5   Cultural Anthropology, Sociology and Social Psychology.

14.18.5.1   Embree, John F., The Japanese. Washington, Smithsonian
            Institute, 1943.

14.19.5.2   - - - "Standardized Error and Japanese Character: A
            Note on Political Interpretation," World Politics, Vol. 2,
            No. 3, April 1950, pp. 439-443.

14.18.5.3   Government Administration Council, Central People's
            Government (China), "Decisions Concerning the Differentiation

of Class Status in the Countryside," Adopted . . . Aug. 4, 1950, People's China, Supplement to Vol. II, No. 8, Oct. 16, 1950.

14.18.5.4 Smythe, H. H., "Note on Racial Ideas of the Japanese," Social Forces, Vol. 31, March 1953, pp. 258-260.

14.18.5.5 - - - and M. M. Smythe, "Race, Culture and Politics in Japan," Phylon, Vol. 13, Sept. 1952, pp. 192-198.

14.18.5.6 Weakland, John H., "The Organization of Action in Chinese Culture," Psychiatry, Vol. 3, No. 3, Aug. 1950, pp. 361-370.

14.18.6 Linguistics and Sociology and Politics of Languages and Scripts.

14.18.6.1 De Francis, John, Nationalism and Language Reform in China. Princeton, Princeton University Press, 1950.

14.18.6.2 Frei, Ernest J., "The Historical Development of the Philippine National Language," Philippine Social Sciences and Humanities Review, Vol. 14, Dec. 1949, pp. 367-400.

14.18.6.3 Hall, R. K., Education for a New Japan. New Haven, Yale University Press, 1949.

14.18.6.4 Hu Shih, The Chinese Renaissance. Chicago, University of Chicago Press, 1934.

14.18.6.5 Isidro, A., et al., Compulsory Education in the Philippines. New York, Unesco, 1952.

14.18.6.6 Swadesh, M., "Nationalism and Language Reform in China," Science and Society, 16 (3), Summer 1952, pp. 273-280.

14.18.6.7 Untalan, Pelagia, Difficulties in the National Language of the Students of the Philippine Normal School. (M.A. Thesis). Manila, University of the Philippines College of Education, 1950. (277 pp.) Mimeographed.

14.18.7 History, General.

14.18.7.1 Ike, Nobutaka, The Beginning of Political Democracy in Japan. Baltimore, Johns Hopkins Press, 1950.

14.18.7.2 Jones, F. C., Japan's New Order in East Asia: Its Rise and Fall 1937-1945. New York, Oxford University Press, 1954.

14.18.7.3 Norman, Herbert E., Japan's Emergence as a Modern State: Political and Economic Problems of the Meiji Period. New York, Institute of Pacific Relations, 1940.

14.18.7.4 - - - Peasant and Soldier in Japan: The Origins of Conscription. New York, Institute of Pacific Relations, 1943.

14.18.7.5 Reischauer, E. O., Japan, Past and Present. New York, Knopf, 1946.

14.18.8   Economic History.

14.18.8.1   Allen, G. C. and A. G. Donnithorne, Western Enterprise in
             Far Eastern Economic Development: China and Japan.
             New York, Macmillan, 1954.

14.18.8.2   Chih-yi, Chang, "China's Population Problem -- A Chinese
             View," Pacific Affairs, Vol. 22, No. 4, December 1949,
             pp. 339-357.

14.18.8.3   Mitchell, Kate Louise, The Industrialization of the Western
             Pacific. New York, Institute of Pacific Relations, 1942.

14.18.8.4   - - - Japan's Industrial Strength. New York, Knopf, 1942.

14.18.9   Economics and Economic Policy.

14.18.9.1   Jenkins, Shirley, American Economic Policy toward the
             Philippines. Stanford, Stanford University Press, 1954.

14.18.10   Geography, Geopolitics and Regional Planning.

14.18.10.1   Cressey, George B., China's Geographic Foundations: A
             Survey of the Land and Its People. New York, McGraw-Hill,
             1934.

14.18.10.2   Roxby, Percy Maude, "China as an Entity: The Comparison
             with Europe," Geography, Vol. 19, Pt. 1, No. 103, March
             1934, pp. 1-20.

14.18.12   Religion and Religious Organizations.

14.18.12.1   Olds, C. B., "Japan Harnesses Religion in the Nation Service,"
             Foreign Affairs, Vol. 21, April 1943, pp. 535-547.

14.18.14   Specific Peoples, Areas and Problems.

14.18.14.1   Fairbank, John King, The United States and China. Cambridge,
             Harvard University Press, 1948.

14.18.14.2   Reischauer, Edwin O., and others, Japan and America Today.
             Stanford, Stanford University Press, 1953.

14.18.14.3   Sansom, Sir George, The Western World and Japan: A
             Study in the Interaction of European and Asiatic Cultures.
             New York, Knopf, 1950.

14.18.14.4   Vinacke, The U. S. and the Far East. Stanford, Stanford
             University Press, 195 .

14.18.14.5   Wiens, H. J., China's March into the Tropics: A Discussion of
             the Southward Penetration of China's Culture, Peoples, and
             Political Control in Relation to the Non-Han-Chinese People of
             South China and in the Perspective of Historical and Cultural
             Geography. Prepared under the auspices of the Office of Naval
             Research. Washington, United States Navy, 1952.

14.19	AFRICA, SOUTH OF THE SAHARA, INCLUDING SUDAN
14.19.1	General Bibliographies and Surveys.
14.19.1.1	African Press and Advertising Annual, 1953-54. (Edited by Charles R. Pask). Cape Town, African Press and Advertising Annual (616 Boston House, Strand St., Cape Town); London, African and Colonial Press Agency, Ltd. (8 Red Lion Sq., London W. C. 1), 1953.
14.19.1.2	Bartlett, Vernon, Struggle for Africa. Rev. Ed., New York, Praeger, 1954.
14.19.1.3	Batten, Thomas Reginald, Problems of African Development. London, Oxford University Press, 1947.
14.19.1.4	Baumann, Hermann, et al., Völkerkunde von Afrika, mit besonderer Berücksichtigung der kolonialen Aufgabe. Essen, Essener Verlagsanstalt, 1940. Written at the peak time of Nazi hopes for colonial expansion.
14.19.1.5	Bourret, F. M., The Gold Coast, A Survey of the Gold Coast and British Togoland, 1919-1951. Stanford, Stanford University Press, 1951.
14.19.1.6	Gunther, John, Inside Africa. New York, Harper, 1955.
14.19.1.7	Hailey, Lord, An African Survey. 2nd ed., London, Oxford University Press, 1945.
14.19.1.8	- - - , Native Administration in the British African Territories. Parts 3 and 4. London, H.M.S.O., 1952.
14.19.1.9	Hellmann, Ellen, ed., Handbook on Race Relations in South Africa. London, Oxford University Press, 1949.
14.19.1.10	Lewis, W. Arthur, Scott, Michael, et al., Attitude to Africa. London, Penguin Books, 1951.
14.19.1.11	Macmillan, W. M., Africa Emergent, Rev. Ed. Harmondsworth, England, Penguin Books, 1949.
14.19.2	General Works on Nationalism.
14.19.2.1	Awolowo, Obafemi, Path to Nigerian Freedom. London, Faber, 1947.
14.19.2.2	Briggs, A., "Nationalism in the Gold Coast," Fortnightly, 1023 and 1024, March and April 1952, pp. 152-157, 231-237.
14.19.2.3	Coleman, James Smoot, Nationalism in Nigeria. Ph.D. Thesis, Harvard University, 1953. (Unpublished.)
14.19.2.4	- - - , "The Problem of Political Integration in Emergent Africa Western Political Quarterly, March 1955, pp. 44-57.
14.19.2.5	- - - , "Current Political Movements in Africa," Annals of the American Academy of Political and Social Science, March 1955, pp. 95-108.

14.19.2.6 - - - , "The Emergence of African Political Parties," Africa Today, ed. Haine, pp. 225-256.

14.19.2.7 - - - , "Nationalism in Tropical Africa," American Political Science Review, June 1954, pp. 404-426.

14.19.2.8 Crabites, P., "Abyssinian Superiority Complex." Catholic World, Vol. 142, Oct. 1935, pp. 10-17.

14.19.2.9 Dundas, C., "African Nationalism," Fortnightly, 1023-1024-1025, 1952, pp. 147-151, 237-243, 307-311.

14.19.2.10 Kenyatta, Jomo, Facing Mount Kenya. London, Secker & Warburg, 1953.

14.19.2.11 Leakey, L. S. B., Mau Mau and the Kikuyu. London, Methuen, 1952.

14.19.2.12 McKay, Vernon, "Nationalism in British West Africa," Foreign Policy Reports, Vol. 24, Mar. 15, 1948, pp. 2-11.

14.19.2.13 Shepperson, G., "Ethiopianism and African Nationalism," Phylon, Vol. 14, March 1953, pp. 9-18.

14.19.2.14 Westermann, Diedrich, "Nationalismus in Afrika," Zeitschrift für Geopolitik, 23 (12), Dec. 1952, pp. 744-751.

14.19.3 Political Science.

14.19.3.1 Apter, David E., The Gold Coast in Transition. Princeton University Press, 1955.

14.19.3.2 Carter, Gwendolyn M., "Can Apartheid Succeed in South Africa?" Foreign Affairs, January 1954, pp. 296-309.

14.19.3.3 - - - , "The Politics of White Supremacy," Annals of the American Academy of Political and Social Science, March 1955, pp. 142-150.

14.19.3.4 Cowan, L. Gray, "Federation for Nigeria," International Journal, Winter 1954-55, pp. 51-60.

14.19.3.5 Davidson, Basil, "The New West Africa," The New Statesman and Nation, Vol. 43, May 3-June 21, 1953, pp. 518-519, 546-547, 667-668, 722-723.

14.19.3.6 Dobie, Edith, "Central African Federation; A Challenge to Principles of British Colonial Policy," World Affairs, Vol. 116, No. 2, Summer 1953, pp. 44-46.

14.19.3.7 Lloyd, Peter C., "The Development of Political Parties in Western Nigeria," The American Political Science Review, September 1955, pp. 693-707.

14.19.3.8 Marquard, L., The Peoples and Policies of South Africa. London, Oxford University Press, 1952. (258 pp.)

14.19.3.9 McCord, J. J., South African Struggle. Pretoria, De Bussy, 1952.

14.19.3.10 Padmore, G., The Gold Coast Revolution: The Struggle of an African People from Slavery to Freedom. London, Dobson, 1953. (272 pp.)

14.19.3.11   Roberts, Michael, and Trollip, E. A. G., The South African Opposition, 1939-45: An Essay in Contemporary History. New York, 1948.

14.19.5   Cultural Anthropology, Sociology and Social Psychology.

14.19.5.1   Balandier, G., "Messianismes et nationalismes en Afrique noire," Cahiers internationaux de sociologie, 14, 1953, pp. 41-65.

14.19.5.2   Bryant, A. T., The Zulu People. Pietermaritzburg, Shuter & Shooter, 1949.

14.19.5.3   Calpin, G. H., There Are No South Africans. London, 1941.

14.19.5.4   - - -, ed., The South African Way of Life. New York, 1954.

14.19.5.5   MacCrane, I. D., Race Attitudes in South Africa. London, Oxford University Press, 1937.

14.19.5.6   Millin, Sarah G., The People of South Africa. New York, Knopf, 1954.

14.19.5.7   Paton, Allan, Cry the Beloved Country: A Story of Comfort in Desolation. New York, Scribner, 1948.

14.19.5.8   - - -, The Land and the People of South Africa. Philadelphia, Lippincott, 1955.

14.19.5.9   Westermann, Diedrich, Autobiographies d'Africains: onze autobiographies d'indigènes originaires de diverses régions de l'Afrique et représentant des métiers et de degrés de culture différents. Paris, Payot, 1943.

14.19.5.10   - - -, The African Today and Tomorrow. London, Oxford University Press, 1939. Includes foreword by the Rt. Hon. Lord Lugard.

14.19.6   Linguistics, Sociology and Politics of Languages and Scripts.

14.19.6.1   Asamoa, E. A., "The Problem of Language in Education in the Gold Coast," Africa, Vol. 25, No. 1, 1955.

14.19.6.2   Barnouw, A. J., Language and Race Problems in South Africa. The Hague, Nijhoff, 1934.

14.19.6.3   Macdougald, Duncan, Jr., The Languages and Press of Africa. Philadelphia, University of Pennsylvania Press, 1944.

14.19.6.4   Malherbe, E. G., The Bilingual School: A Study of Bilingualism in South Africa. London, Longmans, 1946.

14.19.6.5   Pells, E. G., 300 Years of Education in South Africa. Cape Town, Juta, 1954.

14.19.6.6   Union of South Africa, Bureau of Census and Statistics, Census of the Population of the Union of South Africa, enumerated 7th May, 1946. Vol. 4: Languages and Literacy. Pretoria, Government Printer, 1953. Includes "Official languages spoken (all races); home languages (all races); literacy of natives." These figures were delayed seven years between collection and publication.

14.19.6.7　Westermann, Diedrich, "The Study of African Languages: Present Results and Future Needs," Africa (London), Vol. 12, Jan. 1939, pp. 12-26.

14.19.6.8　- - - , and Bryan, M. A., Languages of West Africa. New York, Oxford University Press, 1953.

14.19.7　History

14.19.7.1　Westermann, Diedrich, Geschichte Afrikas: Staatenbildungen südlich der Sahara. Köln, Greven Verlag, 1952.

14.19.9　Economics

14.19.9.1　International Bank for Reconstruction and Development, The Economic Development of Nigeria: Report of a Mission Organized by the International Bank for Reconstruction and Development at the Request of the Governments of Nigeria and the United Kingdom. Baltimore, Johns Hopkins Press, 1955.

14.19.9.2　Munger, E. S., "Economics and African Nationalism," Current History, 25 (143), July -953, pp. 8-13.

14.19.9.3　United Nations, Department of Economic and Social Affairs, Scope and Structure of Money Economies in Tropical Africa. New York, 1955.

14.20   OCEANIA

14.20.3   Political Science.

14.20.3.1 Barnett, A. Campbell, Freedom and Planning in Australia. New York, Hall, 1949; especially, "Nationalism," Ch. 9, pp. 240-266.

INDEX

Berman, Harold Joseph	14.6.3.11
Bertoni, Giulio	14.11.6.1
Beveridge, Sir William	9.6
Bickel, W.	14.10.8.1
Bielstein, H. H.	2.9
Biermann, B.	14.7.11.1
Bigelow, J., see Rosenblueth, A.	4.25
Bingham, Alfred M.	14.3.3.1
Birnie, Arthur	14.3.8.1
Black, Cyril E.; Ed.	14.6.3.12
Bloom, Solomon F.	2.10
Bloomfield, A. I.	9.7
Bloomfield, Leonard	6.3
Blum, Leon	14.7.3.1
Blumenstock, Dorothy, see Lasswell, Harold D.	3.79
Boas, Franz	11.6; 11.7; 11.8
Bodmer, Frederick	6.4
Bogardus, E. S.	5.16; 5.17; 5.18
Bogardus, J. F.	14.3.10.1
Boggs, S. Whittemore	10.1; 10.2
Bomon-Behram, B. K.	14.16.6.3
Bonn, Moritz J.	8.4; 14.2.8.1; 14.12.8.1
Bonne, Alfred	14.15.9.1
Borning, Bernard C.	3.7
Borsody, Stephen, Ed.	14.5.3.1
Boshoff, S. P. E.	14.19.1.2
Boulding, Kenneth E.	9.8, 9.9, 9.10
Bourret, F. M.	14.19.1.2
Bowman, Isaiah	10.3
Bowden, W.	14.3.8.2
Boyd, William Cluser	11.9
Boyd-Orr, John	9.11
Brady, Alexander	14.2.2.2; 14.2.3.1
Brady, Robert A.	8.5; 14.4.3.1

Eldridge, Seba	8.12
Elliott, William Yandell	3.33, 3.34, 3.35, 3.36, 3.37, 3.38
Ellsbree, Willard H.	14.17.2.0
Ellul, J.	12.11
Embree, John F.	14.18.5.1; 14.18.5.2
Emerson, Rupert	3.39, 14.14.2.2; 14.17.2.1; 14.17.3.1a; 14.17.14.1
Engels, Friedrich, see Marx, Karl	9.76
Englert-Faye, Curt	14.10.7.1
Englis, Karel	9.32
Enriques, F.	7.8
Entwistle, W. J.	14.6.6.1; 14.12.6.1
Epstein, F. T.	14.6.1.5
Erickson, Erik H.	14.4.5.2
Eulau, Heintz H. F.	3.40
Eyck, Erich	14.4.7.6; 14.4.7.7
Eysenck, J. J.	5.40
Fainsod, Merle	3.41
Fairbank, John King	14.18.14.1
Fairchild, Henry Pratt	5.41; 5.42; 5.43
Fairgrieve, James	10.10
Fano, R. M.	4.9; 4.10; 4.11
Fay, Sidney B.	7.9; 14.3.7.3; 14.4.7.8
Feder, Gottfried	14.4.3.3
Feiler, A., see also Ascoli, Max	9.33
Feis, Herbert	14.3.8.7
Fellner, E.	5.44
Ferguson, L. W.	5.45
Festinger, L.	4.12
Fife, R. H.	5.46
Finck, Franz Nikolaus	6.8
Finot, Jean	2.24
Firsoff, V. A.	14.3.3.4
Firth, John Rupert	6.9

Haberler, G. F.	9.35
Hacker, Louis M.	14.1.7.9; 14.1.8.4
Hadas, M.	7.10
Haddon, A. C. see Huxley, Julian Sorell	11.23
Hailey, Lord	14.19.1.7; 14.19.1.8
Haldane, J. B. S.	11.15
Haliczer, Josef	14.3.8.8
Hall, R. K.	14.18.6.2
Hall, Robert A.	14.11.6.2
Halvdan, Koht	7.11
Hamilton, Walton	9.36
Hammer, Ellen	14.17.3.2
Hammond, J. L.	14.2.8.12; 14.2.8.13; 14.2.8.14
Hancock, William K.	2.26; 14.2.3.3; 14.2.3.4; 14.2.9.1
Hansen, Alvin H.	9.37; 14.1.9.1
Hansen, H.	2.27
Hantos, Elmer	14.5.3.11
Hanun, M. Theodore Y.	14.5.3.12
Harper, H. R.	5.64
Harris, Abram L.	14.1.8.5
Harris, Seymour E.	9.38; 9.39; 9.40; 14.3.9.4; 14.12.9.2
Harrison, George	14.3.3.7; 14.3.3.8
Hart, Hornell	14.1.5.9
Hartley, E. L., see also Newcomb, T. M.	5.65; 5.139
Hartshorne, Richard	10.13; 10.14
Hatt, Paul K., see William J. Goode	5.60; 9.41
Haugen, Einar I.	6.15
Haugen, William Keith	6.16
Haushofer, Albrecht	10.15
Haushofer, Karl	10.16; 10.17; 10.18; 10.19; 10.20
Havranek, Bohuslav	6.17
Hawtrey, E. G.	9.42; 14.3.9.5

Isaac, Julius	8.52
Isard, Walter	9.52a; 9.53; 9.54; 9.54a
Isidro, A.	14.18.6.5
Issawi, Charles Philip	14.15.9.2
Izzeddin, Nejla	14.15.1.4
Jacobson, Eugene	5.73a
Jaeger, H.	3.62
Jahoda, Marie	1.4; 5.2; 5.120
Jakobson, Roman	6.18; 6.19; 6.20; 6.21; 6.22; 6.23; 6.24
James, Preston E.	10.23; 14.12.10.1
Janowitz, Morris see Shils, Edward A.	14.4.5.11
Janowsky, Oscar I.	2.36
Jászi, Oskar	14.5.3.15; 14.5.3.16; 14.5.3.17; 14.5.7.4
Jenkins, D.	5.74
Jenkins, Shirley	14.18.9.1
Jenks, Leland H.	8.22; 14.12.8.2
Jespersen, Otto	6.25; 6.26
Joachimsen, P.	14.4.7.11
Johansen, Paul	14.4.7.12
Johnson, Charles S.	5.75
Jones, Evan J.	14.2.8.16
Jones, F. C.	14.18.7.2
Jones, Stephen Barr	10.24
Jones, S. W.	14.17.3.3
Jordan P. see Harrison, George	14.3.3.8
Joseph, Alice see Thompson, Laura	5.185
Jouvenel, Bertrand de	3.63
Jurgela, C. R.	14.6.7.8
Kahin, George McTurnan	14.17.2.2

Kluckhohn, Clyde	5.78; 5.79
Knight, Maxwell E.	14.4.3.8
Knight, Sir Henry	14.16.8.2
Knorr, Klaus E.	14.2.7.9
Knupfer, Genevieve, see Lazarsfeld, Paul F.	5.90
Kogan, A. G.	14.5.7.6
Kohn, Hans	1.6; 2.41; 2.42; 2.43; 2.44; 2.45; 2.46; 7.18; 7.19; 7.20; 7.21; 7.22; 13.3; 13.4; 14.2.7.10; 14.4.3.9; 14.4.7.14; 14.4.7.15; 14.4.7.16; 14.4.7.17; 14.4.8.18; 14.4.7.19; 14.4.7.20; 14.5.7.7; 14.6.2.3; 14.6.3.19; 14.6.7.11; 14.6.7.12; 14.6.7.13; 14.6.7.14; 14.7.7.7; 14.15.2.4; 14.15.2.5; 14.15.2.6
Koht, Halvdan	14.9.1.2
Kolnai, Aure	14.5.3.18; 14.5.3.19
Kracauer, Siegfried	14.1.5.14; 14.4.5.5
Krander, E.	12.17
Krech, David	5.80
Kridl, Manfred	14.6.1.7
Kriesberg, Martin	14.1.5.15
Krogman, W. M.	11.26
Kroeber, A. L.	5.81; 5.82; 5.83
Krout, John A.	14.15.3.4
Kučera, Jindrich	6.28a
Kulischer, Eugen	13.5; 14.3.8.10
Kuznets, Simon Smith	9.61; 9.62; 9.63
Ladgham, Bahi	14.15.3.5
Laisay, Michel	14.15.3.6
Lamb, Robert K.	9.64
Lambton, A. K. S.	14.15.5.1
Lamont, Corliss	14.6.2.4
Lampe, J.	2.47
Lamprecht, Karl	14.4.7.21

Schmidt, Peter W.	6.42
Schneefuss, Walter	14.5.7.9
Schueller, Richard, see Gratz, Gustav A.	14.5.8.2
Schuerch, Ernst	14.10.6.3
Schulte, Aloys	8.27
Schuman, Frederick L.	3.144; 3.145; 3.146; 7.29; 7.30; 14.4.3.17; 14.6.3.30
Schumpeter, Joseph	5.168, 5.168a; 9.113, 9.114, 9.115, 9.116
Schwarzenberger, G.	3.147
Scott, Franklin D.	14.9.14
Scotford, J. R.	12.24
Scoville, Warren C.	8.28
Sears, R. R., see Hovland, C. I.	5.71
Seignobos, Charles	14.7.7.9
Sen, B. R.	14.14.2.4
Sestan, E.	
Setälä, E. N.	14.9.6.1
Seton-Watson, Hugh	14.6.3.31; 14.6.7.18
Seton-Watson, Robert William	14.6.7.19; 14.6.7.20
Severson, A. L.	14.1.5.23
Sforza, C.	14.7.3.4
Shafer, Boyd C.	1.10
Shannon, C. E.	4.26; 4.27; 4.28; 4.29; 4.30
Sharma, Rambilas	14.16.6.16
Shaw, C. F.	10.34
Shen, Tsung-lien	14.18.1.4
Shenton, Herbert N.	6.43
Shepherd, William R.	10.35
Shepperson, G.	14.19.2.2
Shils, Edward A., see also Parsons, Talcott	5.145; 5.146; 5.169; 14.4.5.11
Shotwell, James T.	14.4.8.7
Shumeyko, Stephen	14.6.2.5
Shuster, G. N.	14.6.7.21

Vinacke, Harold M.	14.18.14.4
Viner, Jacob	8.38; 9.130; 9.131
Vlekke, Bernhard H. M.	14.8.7.12
Vočadlo, Otakar	6.47
Voegelin, Eric	11.37
Von Foerster, Heinz	4.31
Von Neumann, John and Oskar, Morgenstern	9.132
Von Rutkowski, Lother Stengel	2.60
Von Wartburg, Walter	6.49; 7.34; 14.7.6.3; 14.11.6.3; 14.11.6.4
Vossler, Karl	6.48
Vossler, Otto	7.32
Vucinich, Alexander	14.6.9.2
Wade-Evans, A. W.	14.2.7.14
Waehler, M.	14.4.5.13
Wallas, Graham	3.161
Walsh, Gerald Groveland, S. J.	7.33
Wambaugh, Sarah	3.162; 14.7.3.6
Ward, Sir Adolphus William, and Gooch, G.P.	14.2.7.15
Ward, B.	14.5.3.30
Ware, Caroline	5.193
Warfel, Harry R.	14.1.7.16
Warner, William Lloyd	14.1.5.26; 14.1.5.27; 14.1.5.28; 14.1.5.29
Wayne, Ivor, see McGranahan, Donald G.	5.108
Weakland, John H.	5.194; 14.18.5.6
Weaver, W., see Shannon, C. E.	4.30
Weber, Alfred	9.133
Weber, Max (5)	8.9; 5.195; 5.196; 5.197; 8.39; 9.134
Webster, C. K.	14.2.7.16
Wecter, Dixon	14.1.7.17
Weerawardana, I. D. S.	14.16.6.17

Zinner, Paul E.	14.6.3.36
Zipf, George K.	2.69; 4.37
Zischka, Antoine	14.15.1.6
Znaniecki, Florian, see also Thomas, W. I.	1.20; 5.182; 5.203
Zollner, Erich	7.36
Zoltowski, Adam	14.6.1.10

16

ع